The Russian Empire about 1900

© Rand McNally & Co., R.L. 83-5-46

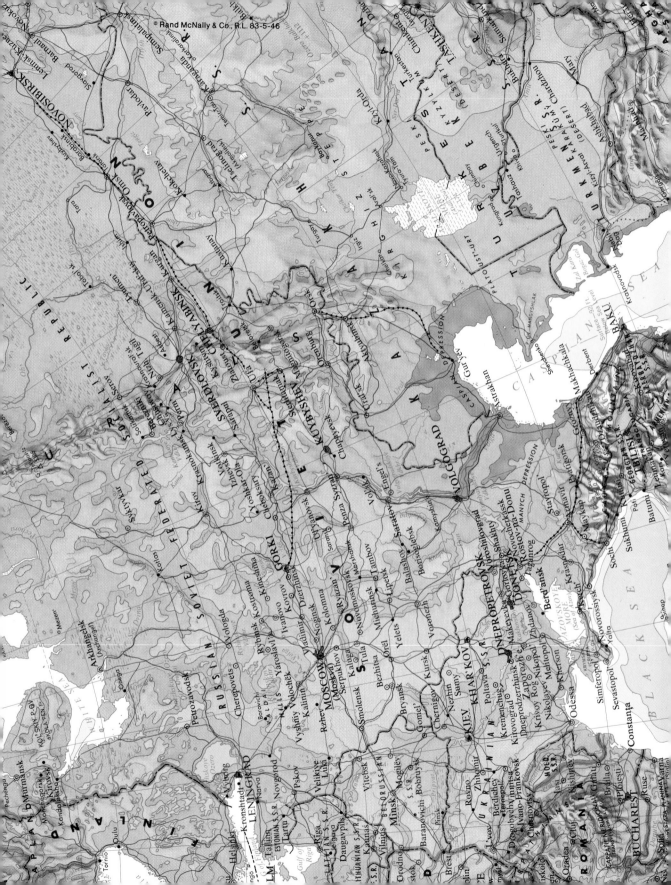

Enchantment of the World

RUSSIA

A History to 1917

By Abraham Resnick

Consultants: Professor John Bushnell, Ph.D., Assistant Professor of History, Northwestern University, Evanston, Illinois and Professor Irwin Weil, Ph.D., Professor of Russian and Russian Literature, Northwestern University, Evanston, Illinois

Consultant for Social Studies: Donald W. Nylin, Ph.D., Assistant Superintendent for Instruction, Aurora West Public Schools, Aurora, Illinois

Consultant for Reading: Robert L. Hillerich, Ph.D., Bowling Green State University, Bowling Green, Ohio

CHILDRENS PRESS, CHICAGO

This woman is wearing the Ukrainian national costume.

For my daughter Gina Irene Resnick

Library of Congress Cataloging in Publication Data

Resnick, Abraham.
  Russia, a history to 1917.

  (Enchantment of the world)
  Includes index.
  Summary: A history of the largest country in the
world, from early days to 1917.
  1. Soviet Union—History—Juvenile literature.
[1. Soviet Union—History] I. Title. II. Series.
DK41.R37 1983   947   83-7369
ISBN 0-516-02785-9   AACR2

Picture Acknowledgments
Gladys J. Peterson: Pages 4, 5, 8, 28, 30 (2 photos), 33
(top), 41 (right), 52 (right), 66 (bottom)
Worldwide Photo Specialty, Alexander M. Chabe: Cover,
pages 6 (2 photos), 9, 10, 13, 19 (2 photos), 20 (2 photos),
26, 36 (left), 40, 41 (left), 47, 52 (left), 59 (2 photos), 63
(2 photos), 65, 66 (top), 69, 75 (left), 80 (top middle and
right, bottom), 90 (top), 95 (left and center), 96, 97, 98
(bottom), 104, 107 (left)
**State Museums of the Moscow Kremlin, Photographed
by Sheldan Collins, The Metropolitan Museum of Art:**
Pages 16, 24, 31, 33 (bottom left and right), 34, 42
(2 photos), 48, 56, 64
Society for Cultural Relations with the USSR: Pages 36
(right), 53, 54 (3 photos), 61, 79, 98 (top), 108 (3 photos),
110 (2 photos)
**The Metropolitan Museum of Art, Gift of the
Humanities Fund, Incorporated, 1972:** Page 70
Colour Library International: Page 93
Historical Pictures Service, Chicago: Pages 71, 75 (right),
80 (top left), 90 (bottom), 95 (right)
**Novosti Press Agency Publishing House, Moscow,
USSR:** Pages 88 (2 photos), 89 (2 photos)
**Metropolitan Museum of Art, Gift of Mrs. Henry
Morgenthau, 1933:** Page 107 (right)
Len Meents: Maps on pages 7, 26, 38, 61, 103
**Courtesy Flag Research Center, Winchester,
Massachusetts 01890:** Flag on back cover
Cover: St. Basil's Church in Moscow

Many of the first Russian churches were built of wood.

TABLE OF CONTENTS

Chapter 1 Mother Russia (An Introduction)..... *7*

Chapter 2 Russia's Early Years (Prehistory to the 800s)..... *11*

Chapter 3 Formation of the Russian State (800 to the 1200s)..... *17*

Chapter 4 Russia Under the Mongol Yoke (1223 to the 1400s)..... *25*

Chapter 5 The Russian Orthodox Church (The 1400s to the 1500s)..... *29*

Chapter 6 Russian Heroes or Russian Villains (1240 to 1584)..... *35*

Chapter 7 Russia's Time of Troubles (1584 to 1613)..... *43*

Chapter 8 New Beliefs and "Old Believers" (The 1600s to the 1650s)..... *49*

Chapter 9 The Russian Serfs (The Middle Ages to 1775)..... *51*

Chapter 10 Peter the Great (1682 to 1725)..... *57*

Chapter 11 Catherine the Great (1762 to 1796)..... *67*

Chapter 12 Tsar Paul, Tsar Alexander, and Napoleon (1796 to 1825)..... *73*

Chapter 13 The Decembrist Rebels and Tsar Nicholas I (1825 to 1855)..... *81*

Chapter 14 Expansion in Asia (1558 to 1905)..... *85*

Chapter 15 Alexander II, Nicholas II, and the Road to Revolution (1855 to 1905)..... *91*

Chapter 16 Resisters, Rivals, and Revolutionaries (1904 to 1917)..... *99*

Chapter 17 Russia's Contribution to the Arts..... *105*

Mini-Facts at a Glance..... *112*

Index..... *122*

Summers in Russia are short. Melting snows from atop the Caucasus Mountains feed this river (above). Winters are cold and long in most places. A horse pulls a sleigh, one means of transportation in the winter (below).

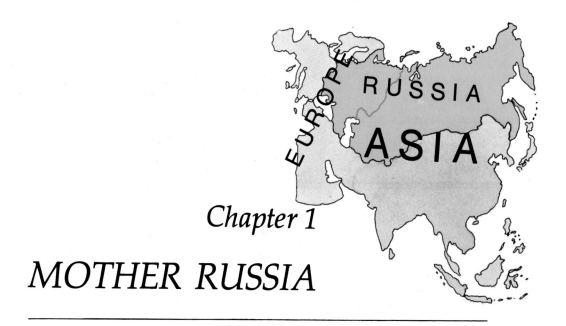

Chapter 1

MOTHER RUSSIA

RUSSIA'S SYMBOL

Nations have always made great use of symbols to rally strong feelings of love of country. Russia has adopted a family member as a symbol—"Mother Russia."

The exact image of "Mother Russia" remains a mystery. Her appearance must have been determined by her land features and the great historical events that took place on them. Yet she has changed much over the years.

"Mother Russia" is big! Even as a "child," she was considered oversized. She grew rapidly. Today, she is the largest country in the world. "Mother Russia" has made her home in eastern Europe and most of northern Asia. Her many children are widely scattered throughout her vast territory. Hundreds of Russian rivers have helped transport her family east to China and south to the borders of Persia, 2,000 miles (3,218 kilometers) away. The

Listvyanka, a village on Lake Baikal

river waterways routed the early nomadic tribes and later hunters, tradesmen, gold-seeking adventurers, and the exiled to the endless eastern frontiers. When Siberia was opened for settlement, its 6,000-mile (9,654-kilometer) stretch of steppe (open prairie) lands, forests, and mountains from Europe to the Pacific Ocean became "Mother Russia's" and came under her influence and rules.

"Mother Russia" is old! Her ancestry can be traced back to the Stone Age. Her face is weatherbeaten and worn, brought on by long, bitterly cold winter seasons of dreariness and decay. Russia has always been the record holder for the coldest inhabited place in the world.

"Mother Russia" appears strong and hearty. She is most likely of peasant stock, conditioned to laboring in the out-of-doors. Her hands have felt the fertile black earth of the village farms. Years of hard work in the sun and wind have reddened her complexion. Her great-grandmothers of centuries past had to work even harder. Many were serfs who were forced against their will to

A painting by Ilya Repin (1844-1930) is entitled Religious Procession to Kursk Guverniya.

work for landlords. Serfs were tillers of the soil. They had little freedom and little to show for their efforts.

"Mother Russia's" cheeks are full. Large portions of starchy foods like breads, cereals, and potatoes have helped to round them out. She remembers, however, past droughts and famines that caused malnutrition and starvation. The problems of ownership of land and distribution of food have led to centuries of unrest.

"Mother Russia" is probably a descendant of the East Slavic peoples, the early settlers considered the forefathers of the Russians. But, since hordes of invaders were able to gain entry into Russia with ease, it is likely that her ancestors included other groups besides the Slavs. Her face shows a mixture of many faces from many places.

We need to know much more about "Mother Russia's" life — from her early days to 1917 — if we are to understand her. She is a very interesting lady. She has many experiences to relate. She has lived through a very exciting period of our world's history.

Birch trees on the outskirts of Moscow

Chapter 2

RUSSIA'S EARLY YEARS

Throughout much of Russia the land a few feet below the surface is permanently frozen, except for a brief period during the summer months. The old roots of trees, unable to penetrate deep into the ice, tend to spread out in many different directions far from their trunks. The roots are not firmly fixed, but they draw water and food from various sources.

Russia, like the trees of her forests, also has ancient and far-reaching roots. The origin of the word *Russia* is not clear. Some historians think it came from the Greek, after a tribe that lived in southern Russia. Others claim that the term stems from a German town or once was a Finnish word.

NOMADIC TRIBES

Hundreds of years before Russia became a state and eventually a kingdom, many nomadic tribes in search of fresh grazing land wandered into the fertile steppe region of southern Russia. Some tribes were attracted by new hunting grounds or the great streams and rivers for fishing. As each tribe increased, finding food became a matter of survival. Brutal raids and tribal wars were carried out in order to gain control of land, to steal supplies, or to capture enemies and make them servants.

The Scythians, the earliest inhabitants of Russia, were one such tribe. They came to the south Russian steppe about seven hundred years before the birth of Christ. The Scythians were nomads who once lived in southwestern Asia in a land now known as Iran. They were considered an Indo-European people, but their language was similar to Persian.

SETTLEMENTS

The Greeks, who built trading settlements along the northern shores of the Black Sea, tried to trade with the Scythians. Furs, honey, and slaves were exchanged for ornaments, utensils, fabrics, perfumes, and weapons. Sometimes strong tribal rulers would demand tribute, or a tax, from weaker tribes. Payments would assure that the weaker tribes would not be destroyed or raided. Trading with the Scythians was difficult. The Greeks, and later the Romans, regarded the Scythians as cruel barbarians.

As time passed, many other people began to migrate into the Russian forestlands as well as the steppe region. Each group brought its own skills and customs to Russia.

THE GOTHS

The Greeks were excellent tradesmen who introduced civilized ways of living. The Roman legions introduced ideas about

The Caucasus Mountains are on the east side of the Black Sea.

construction and military organizaton. In the first and second centuries A.D. a change occurred with the arrival of Germanic tribes. These tribes, called the Goths, tended to settle in a set place rather than wander over large territories. They obeyed their princes and kings. The Goths followed the rules of their villages and provinces, making it easy to establish their kingdom and an orderly form of government over much of western Russia. They were the first tribes on Russian soil to accept the Christian faith.

INVADERS

The achievements of the Goths were ruined in the fourth century with the arrival of the Huns, who expelled them. The Huns were powerful nomadic hordes, considered Turko Mongols, who originated in north central Asia. They invaded southern Russia and later set up an empire there and in central Europe. The Huns captured many people and made them their subjects. If they refused to provide the Huns with food and tribute, they were severely oppressed, tortured, or killed. Many prisoners were sold to the Romans for large sums of money. The most famous of the Hun leaders was the feared and hated Attila, a wild terrorist who murdered his own brother in order to gain power.

Eventually oppression by the Huns was halted. They were replaced by other groups, some more warlike than others. The Turks, who were fine cavalrymen, charged into Russia in the sixth century. The Khazars, a unique Turkish tribe, arrived in the eighth century and settled in the vicinity of the mouth of the Volga River. They adopted the Jewish religion, were exceptional tradesmen, and lived in south Russia peacefully for many years. Far to the east the Kirghiz made inroads into Russia, too. They were a wild and remote people who made interesting death masks (casts taken from the faces of the dead).

THE BULGARS AND THE SLAVS

The Bulgars settled the middle Volga area. Some moved west to the Balkans where the word *Bulgar* probably led to the naming of Bulgaria. A strange forest group, they lived by hunting and trapping in the southern mountains of Russia. They primarily practiced the primitive religion of Shamanism. Like the American Indians of long ago, they relied on a shaman, or medicine man, to explain the unseen world of gods, demons, ancestral spirits, and animal powers. Many of these mountain people may have moved eastward to roam the vast Siberian interior. Others moved westward.

A group of mobile people were the Slavs. Their descendants now inhabit Russia. It is impossible to determine where in Russia the first settlement of these Slavs was made. Some think they originated northeast of the Carpathian Mountains. Repeated invasions of their lands by Asiatic hordes pushed them west. Like most tribes in that region, they were rovers, but once the occupation of their homeland weakened, they returned to settle large parts of eastern Europe. By the 800s the eastern Slavs established themselves around three great centers—Kiev in the southwest, Novgorod in the north, and Tmutarakan in the southeast. They mingled freely with the people living in these sections, particularly with the Finns, Germans, and Turks. They became peaceful, but quarreling, farmers, living as clans in stockade villages. Their numbers increased greatly and they began to spread out over their vast homeland.

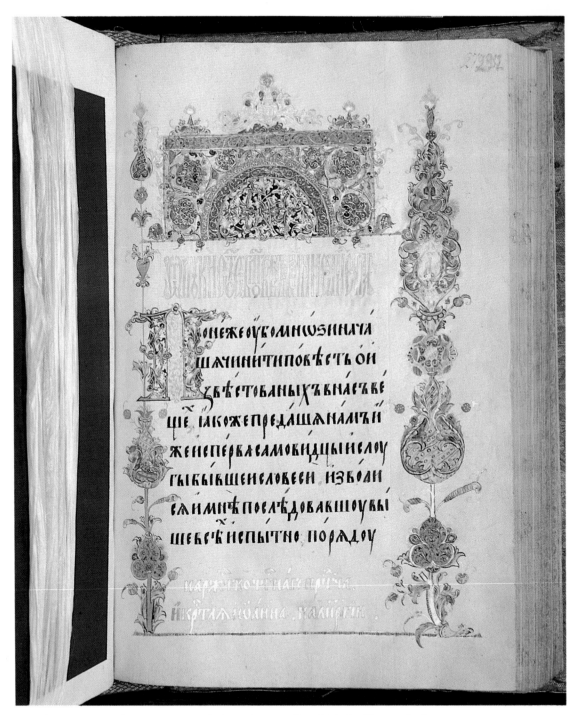

In order to convert the Russians to Christianity, Cyril and Methodius worked out an alphabet, which eventually was called Cyrillic.

Chapter 3

FORMATION OF THE RUSSIAN STATE

Two events in the ninth century had a great influence on Russian history. Both helped unite the Slavic tribes and form the Russian state. And both helped pave the way for the adoption of Christianity in Russia.

CYRIL AND METHODIUS

At that time in Constantinople, the ancient capital of the Byzantine Empire now known as Istanbul, there was one united Catholic church. Two brothers, Cyril and Methodius, were Christian missionaries whose mission was to make the Slavic people Christians. In order to reach the Slavs, they had to use their native language. They worked out an alphabet based upon Greek letters, which eventually was called Cyrillic, and began to translate church books into the new language. That language, though changed some over the years, is still used by all Slavs belonging to the Eastern church. The Slavic language written in Russia today stems from the efforts of Cyril and Methodius over a thousand years ago.

THE VIKINGS

The second great event that helped unify the Slavs came from Scandinavia. Pirates and traders known as Vikings or Varangians sailed their armed boats down the rivers toward Constantinople. Their princes brought along armies of hired soldiers called mercenaries. Many were merchant warriors who helped collect tribute. The Slavs benefited by having new open trade routes to the south. They began to cooperate with the Northmen who brought safety and order to the trading towns along their riverbanks.

Rurik, the leader of the Vikings, governed Novgorod. For many years Novgorod was one of the most powerful cities of Russia as well as one of the richest. But it was too far north to become the center of the early Russian state.

Rurik's successor, Oleg, combined the northern and southern trading centers into a loosely organized state with a central authority at Kiev. The area was soon to be brought into "Russian" hands and the formation of Rus (Russia) was underway, with Oleg as its founder. The year 882 is traditionally regarded as the date of the foundation of the ancient Russian state.

CHRISTIANITY

In the years following, a very lively trade developed between Russia and the Byzantine Empire. Russian merchants observed new ways of living during their trading excursions to Constantinople. Most of the Kiev Russians were pagans. Legend says the visitors to Constantinople became interested in learning about Christianity. Upon their return to Kiev, they brought back

Above left: Vladimir I brought Christianity to Kiev. Above right: The remains of the Golden Gate of Kiev built in the 1000s

more than mere goods to trade. Apparently many of the tradesmen had found religion and were eager to "sell" it to others as well.

Once Christianity was introduced in Russia it was adopted by many of the poor people. Life was hard. Serfs and servants dreamed of a better life in the hereafter. For those forced to work the land from sunup to sundown, Christianity offered a ray of hope for their suffering.

In 988 Vladimir I, the ruler of Kiev, became a Christian. He had first examined the faiths of the Jews, of the Roman Catholics, and of the Mohammedans. It is said that he chose Greek Orthodoxy rather than Roman Catholicism because of the close relationship between Kiev and Constantinople.

Now Kiev and the Russians shared a common culture and a common language.

MOTHER OF RUSSIAN CITIES

Changes were beginning to take place in Kiev, the city that

In the Cathedral of St. Sophia in Kiev are beautiful frescoes (above left), which were painted on freshly spread plaster before it dried. The tomb of Prince Yaroslav the Wise (above right)

developed along the bank of the Dnieper River. Ancient Kiev was to become the "mother of Russian cities" and capital of the powerful early Russian state known as Kievan Rus. With the rise of Christianity, golden-domed churches were built throughout the city. The largest of all was the splendid Cathedral of St. Sophia, built more than nine hundred years ago in the reign of Prince Yaroslav the Wise.

SEEDS OF DISCONTENT

There were other changes as well. The Slavs began to use plows. They became better farmers. The yields of their crops increased. Some of the villages in Russia grew into fortresslike towns surrounded by high log walls and barrier ditches known as moats. Townspeople farming outside the walls of a town had to scurry back each evening before the drawbridge over the moat was raised and the city gates were shut. There was always the threat of a sudden attack by an enemy. Soldiers, wearing armor plates and steel helmets, armed with swords and spears, would stand guard at the gate towers.

Along the river wharves merchant ships from different countries docked with cargoes of vases, gold and silver jewelry, colorful silks, wines, and dried fruit. Some farmers grew rich as farming and livestock breeding developed and private ownership of property appeared. Often the rich were the nobility. They were princes and boyars, a privileged class of aristocrats just below that of the ruling princes. The boyars frequently used their power to seize more and more land. They were able to make the poorer peasants and craftsmen work for them.

There were great differences between the lives of the upper and lower classes. A prince, with his boyars and trusted warriors, would feast on the finest foods and costly wines. Plates were often made of gold or silver. Servants cooked and served the meals. Musicians called boyans (minstrels) provided background music on ancient stringed instruments. The upper-class men wore tailor-made caftans, which were long-sleeved gowns fastened by a belt at the waist. Dark capes and fur-trimmed hats were used as outer wear. Personal jewelers and goldsmiths made candlestick holders, goblets, rings, and bracelets of precious metals. Cobblers made soft high boots of goatskin, usually dyed red. The palaces and noblemen's homes were made comfortable by fireplaces, oak tables, and oriental rugs.

The poor, the servants, and the peasants experienced none of the good life of the nobility. Living conditions for the lower classes were wretched. Their quarters consisted of cold, dark, smoke-filled, dirt-floor huts with bare furnishings. Their clothing was often wet, soiled, and tattered. Boots were usually in need of repair. Food was scarce. Sickness and disease were common.

The power of the nobility and ruling classes increased. The lower classes felt they were being taken advantage of by the more privileged members of Russian society. The seeds of discontent between the landowners and the peasants, the boyars and the workers, began to grow.

GROWTH OF KIEV

During the great days of the Kievan Rus, two rulers contributed to its growth and prosperity. Prince Yaroslav the Wise (1019-1054) helped start schools and libraries, had books translated, and was a patron of art and music. He beautified Kiev by building a palace and churches. During his reign the preparation of the first code of Russian laws was begun. The laws dealt with theft, inheritance, and usury (the practice of lending money at very high rates of interest).

Yaroslav improved the status of women. He helped centralize the government. In foreign relations he was able to achieve recognition for Russia. Yaroslav himself was married to a Swedish princess; his sister was married to the Polish king; three daughters were married to the kings of France, Hungary, and Norway; and a son married into the Greek imperial family.

Vladimir II, born Vladimir Monomach in 1053, was a grandson of both Yaroslav the Wise and the Byzantine Emperor Constantine. He was considered an ideal ruler during his reign from 1113 to 1125. Today he is regarded as old Kiev's last great man. After a period of vicious civil wars and feuds, he succeeded to the throne at the age of sixty and helped reunite the country.

DECLINE OF KIEV

Kiev, after three hundred years of being Russia's Grand Principality, started to decline after the death of Vladimir Monomach. There were a number of causes. Jealous princes continued to fight over power and riches. Differences arose as to who should succeed to the throne when a prince of Kiev died. Foreign raiders began to disrupt Kiev traders and move in on the fertile farming lands of the region. Foreign trade with Constantinople declined when the Crusaders attacked the city. Tremendous loss of life due to repeated wars lowered the productivity and growth of the area. Finally, emigration toward the northwest, southwest, and northeast began to take place. Kiev was starting to compete with Novgorod, a city in the far northwest with a lively trade in fur and forest products with growing European nations.

A shift of power, wealth, and population from Kievan Rus to the northeast river valleys around the towns of Suzdal, Vladimir, and Moscow did much to change the course of Russian history as well. Subdivision of the Russian people, characterized by differences of language and culture, into Great Russians, Little Russians (Ukrainians), and White Russians (Byelorussians) began to spring up. New political centers and small principalities with strong local governments emerged. Russian colonization was about to reach out into a new "land of villages." But still the Russian princes continued to fight destructive wars among themselves. They were badly weakened by civil wars during the 1200s. No strong central control was established. The Russians were about to pay a heavy price for their selfish princely feuds and divisions.

The only city spared when the Mongols invaded Russia was Novgorod. This painting, called Our Lady of Tenderness, *was painted in Novgorod in the twelfth century.*

Chapter 4

RUSSIA UNDER THE MONGOL YOKE

The Mongols, later known as Tatars, penetrated Russia for almost 250 years beginning in 1223. The Mongols were a fierce tribe of horsemen who moved out of northern Asia and swept across Russia and Europe, destroying everything in their path. The Mongol raiders first looted, then put the torch to Russian cities, made the princes pay them heavy taxes, and took thousands of captured Russians as slaves.

The Mongols were the best soldiers in the world at this time. Their army was organized by "decimals," in units of 10, 100, 1,000, and 10,000. Terrorism was their tactic and slaughter was their strategy. Loyalty was demanded and traitors were few. Nothing could stop them. They had great generals who relied upon military intelligence, spies, and advance scouting parties before attacking.

The Mongols trained their horses to withstand the Siberian snow and cold. Mongol soldiers could shoot arrows from horseback while charging at blazing speeds.

The Mongol tribes rarely built permanent homes. Their encampments of felt tents could be folded quickly and carried with them. Their women and children followed wherever they went. The huge Mongol army became known as the Golden Horde because one of their early leaders, Batu Khan (ruler), a

RUSSIA IN 1360
——— Russia's Border Today

*A helmet worn by the Russians at
the time of the invasion of the Golden Horde.*

grandson of Genghis Khan, lived in a magnificent gold-colored tent. The tent, twenty feet (six meters) around, was set on four oversized wheels and drawn by two dozen massive oxen.

VICIOUS WARFARE

The Mongols were vicious in warfare. They often celebrated victories on the battlefield by feasting and dancing upon boards laid over their captives. The prisoners either suffocated or were crushed to death. They were known to use captives, especially old men, women, and children, as a front-line screen while advancing against their foe.

Shortly after their first victory in the Battle of the River Kalka, north of the Sea of Azov, the Golden Horde invaded central Russia. In one month it captured and burned fourteen cities, including Moscow. In 1240 tens of thousands of Mongols sacked Kiev.

MOSCOW PRINCES

It was unusual for the Mongols to remain in one place for a long period of time. They left officers and special tax collectors in the Russian cities to gather in their tribute. The princes of Moscow were the best tax collectors of all. Since the Mongols were primarily interested in getting yearly taxes, they let the Moscow princes run things on their own. Little by little the Moscow princes became the leaders of Russia. Collecting taxes became one of their most important tasks. They stashed away huge piles of money in secret hiding places in the Kremlin, which was a citadel—a fortress within the city of Moscow. Ivan I, who reigned as grand prince of Moscow from 1325 to 1340, was nicknamed Ivan the Moneybag because he was so successful at tax collecting.

One prince of Moscow had a different interest. He was Dmitry, who in 1380 got up enough courage to go to battle against the Mongols near the river Don. Dmitry was a modern general. He taught his troops to use firearms against an enemy armed only with spears, swords, axes, and bows and arrows. Although their battering rams, fire missiles, and assault towers were good for combating fortresses, the Mongols were now faced with a new type of warfare. The Mongol invaders returned and the Russians continued to pay them taxes, but the hero Dmitry showed his fellow Russians that the Mongols could be beaten.

LESSONS LEARNED FROM THE MONGOLS

In 1453 Constantinople was captured by the Turks. As a Christian religious center it was often called "the second Rome." Now many church leaders and educated people fled to Moscow,

In 1367 Prince Dmitry began construction of the Kremlin in Moscow. This is one of the churches in the Kremlin.

which became known as "the third Rome." It was the responsibility of the grand prince of Moscow to protect Christianity against nonbelievers in the name of the Russian Orthodox church. This became a very special cause of the crown.

The Golden Horde remained powerful for many years, but many changes came about during its conquest of Russia. Taxation became the normal way of supporting those in power. The influence of Chinese and other Asiatic civilizations was introduced into Russian culture in the form of words, customs, cruelty towards slaves, financial practices, administration, and the acceptance of emperors and ruling classes.

The Mongols taught the Russians much about governing and fighting. Novgorod alone became an important commercial center as much of the rest of the Russian economy declined. Yet, Moscow, with the advantage of having only five ruling princes over a period of two hundred years, experienced steady growth and showed a potential for greatness.

Chapter 5

THE RUSSIAN
ORTHODOX CHURCH

Like earlier nomad conquerors, the Mongols were fairly tolerant of the church in Russia. For the most part they did not interfere in religious matters. They didn't even bother to collect taxes from the church or its clergy. Many churches and monasteries, especially those in and around Moscow, were able to grow rich and powerful. Some churchmen became the greatest of all Russian landowners.

The Eastern church chose to be recognized as the Orthodox church. It was controlled by the patriarchs of Constantinople until 1448. (Patriarchs are "father-rulers" of the Orthodox church. Other high-ranking officials are metropolitans, who are heads of districts, and archbishops, who are the leaders of individual churches.) The Orthodox church bishops taught that their faith was the "true belief," a term that came from the Greek words *orthe* and *doxa.*

During the Middle Ages the Russian Orthodox church took on considerable authority. It gave the people a feeling of belonging, of having something in common. This did much to bring the

The old churches had tall onion-shaped domes. Icons, paintings of Christ, the Virgin, and the saints, were carried in processions.

Russian people together. The church was to become a very important part of their lives. At church they found peace and harmony and would stay for hours. Some churches were adorned with precious gems or rare jewels. It was enjoyable to pray and become familiar with the services.

THE FIRST RUSSIAN CHURCHES

Most early Russian churches were simple wooden structures. A number were built without the use of a single nail. They all had interesting onion-shaped domes and were usually the most visible, if not the highest, landmarks for miles around. There were no seats inside except for a few side chairs for the very old. People would wander in and out and either stand or kneel to pray. The men occupied the right portion of the church and the women

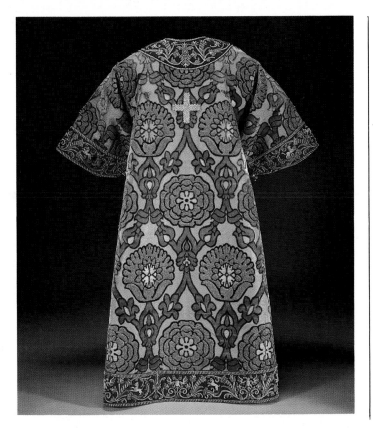

*Bishop's vestment
made of velvet
embroidered with pearls*

assembled to the left. The only light was furnished by the countless candles burned during the prayers of the worshipers. Paintings of Christ, the Virgin, and patron saints were displayed on gold-colored screens and icons. The big icons were carried in prayer processions. Since there were no statues in Russian churches, the painted pictures became holy images for the faithful churchgoers to focus on during their meditations. Most would approach the holy images with low bows of reverence, or they might bend to the floor, face down, as a token act of worship.

The priests were clothed in rich, full-length robes often embroidered in gold and silver. Their headgear was styled like 6-inch (152-millimeter) high flowerpots turned upside down. Higher ranking clergy wore veillike head coverings that fell backward over the shoulders. The miters, or tall caps, of the bishops and patriarchs often glittered with jewels. Picture representations of the saints hung from gold chains around their necks. They rarely appeared without their traditional patriarchal staffs, the emblem of their authority. At that time all Orthodox priests wore beards, to emulate Christ and the fathers of the church.

THE MONK SERGIUS

The Russian church in the fourteenth century helped to civilize the great mass of people. Those of the clergy who led truly Christian lives were deeply respected. Some, like Sergius, a humble monk, settled the feuds of princes and gave courage to soldiers and hope to the downtrodden. In those days many monks worked the land to stay alive. As men who had taken religious vows to live apart from the world, they were always seeking some remote "wilderness" in which to start a secluded colony. Sergius founded the great Monastery of the Trinity in the forest northeast of Moscow. Other monks started additional monasteries. Soon families began to settle nearby in order to enjoy the protection of the monastery and the fruits of the hard-laboring monks. In time the peasants began to work for the monks. Before long they became tenants, paying the monastery for the use of the land. In that way they became indebted to the church. Then some of the monks, unhappy with this turn of events, would move to a new location far from people, only to see the same process start over again. This movement of monks and families throughout the land helped spread religious influences and the Russian peasant way of life from the White Sea to the Black Sea and eastward to the Ural Mountains.

Above: The interior of a Russian Orthodox church in Odessa. Below left: A silver chalice made in 1586, used by the clergy. Below right: A satin veil embroidered with gold and silk threads, made in the sixteenth century, shows St. John the Evangelist reading the Gospels.

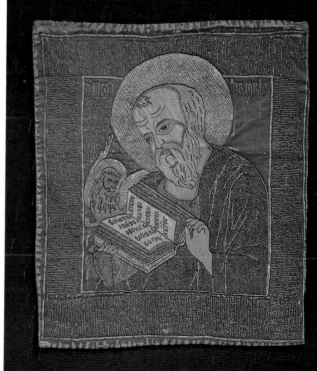

*Ivan the Terrible presented these altar Gospels to the
Cathedral of the Annunciation in the Moscow Kremlin in 1568.*

Chapter 6

RUSSIAN HEROES OR RUSSIAN VILLAINS

During the Mongol era, which ended in the late 1400s, the Renaissance was taking place in Western Europe. It was a transitional movement between the medieval and modern periods and was marked by a great revival of learning and classical art. But under Mongol control, Russia was cut off from these important Western influences. She was going through a different kind of change. Russia was growing up. She was beginning to test her strength against others. She was becoming self-reliant and independent. She was experimenting and was easily influenced.

ALEXANDER OF NOVGOROD

As a young country, Russia's image of herself was greatly uplifted by the heroics of Alexander of Novgorod. He, too, was young, when at twenty years of age in 1240 he and a small band of warriors defeated a force of crusading Swedish knights at the Neva River. Prince Alexander came to be known as Alexander Nevsky, which means Alexander of the Neva. The victory considerably strengthened Russia's defenses in the north. Two years later Alexander Nevsky met an army of Teutonic knights on

Left: A painting of Alexander Nevsky. Right: An artist's impression
of The Battle on the Ice from sixteenth century chronicles

the ice of Lake Chudskoye. These German crusaders were bent on plundering the eastern shores of the Baltic Sea. Theirs was a holy war against Orthodox Russians who refused to be converted to Roman Catholicism.

The Battle on the Ice proved to be one of Russia's greatest victories and made Alexander one of the holy names of medieval Russia. Today he remains a patriotic hero for his courage and cleverness in defeating the German army. With a quickly assembled array of artisans, peasants, and merchants to bolster his troops, Alexander took on the highly trained and experienced Teutonic knights. He knew the knights would advance in a wedge-shaped formation against the center of the Russian regiments. Alexander decided to trick the enemy. He put his best foot soldiers and cavalry on the sides and to the rear. He placed his fast, lightly armed archers at a position up front and center to take the first charge of the heavily armed enemy. His own choice battle-scarred battalion of bodyguards was hidden behind a cliff in the forest.

The battle began with a flying wedge of German cavalry striking deep into the Russian center. It was so easy for them to advance that they thought victory was at hand. They began to celebrate and cheer after a few minutes of battle. Nevsky then led his mounted troops in a flank charge from his strong side, while the peasant mob attacked the knights from the other flank. Then the largest part of the Russian army attacked from the rear, on foot. The Teutonic formation broke up as soon as Alexander's hidden soldiers appeared in force. The Germans' horses stumbled and slipped on the ice. Since the battle occurred in April, much of the ice was thin. It started to crack and melt beneath the heavy weight of the armored horsemen. Many knights fell through the ice and sank to the bottom of the lake. Four hundred knights died there. The rest of the survivors fled or were taken as prisoners back to Novgorod, lashed to their own horses. The eastward drive of the Teutonic knights was halted. The Russians lost many men during the fighting, but gained something they urgently needed at the time—a true national hero, Alexander Nevsky.

IVAN III

Ivan III, the grand prince of Moscovy (Moscow), was one of the founders of the unified Russian state. At the height of his rule he

RUSSIA IN 1524

—— Russia's Border Today

boldly took on the title of "Autocrat of All Russia." He came to the throne of Moscow at age twenty-two in 1462. His first goal was to reconquer from Poland-Lithuania the Ukrainian possessions of his forefathers. Ivan was not fast moving. Many thought he was a coward. By war strategy, tact, and diplomacy he managed to triple the size of Russia's territory. But that took forty-three years.

Before Ivan could overcome his enemies to the west at the frontiers with Lithuania and Poland, he needed to absorb prosperous neighboring Novgorod with its vast regional empire. Ivan knew that Novgorod could not grow enough food to feed its population. He also knew that she relied on trade with western allies, including German merchants. There was also growing disunity in Novgorod. The Orthodox religion opposed the Catholics. The moneyed class was at odds with the workmen and tradesmen. The city was divided. Some wanted closer ties with Moscow, while others wanted to cast their lot with Catholic Poland and Lithuania. Ivan knew that these disagreements would weaken Novgorod's will to fight. So, as usual, Ivan was patient. He waited six years (1471-1477) to bring the city to subjection, mostly by cutting off its incoming food supply. Thousands of nearly starving Novgorod natives were then sent to central Russia and replaced by settlers from Moscow.

SPREADING THE RUSSIAN BORDERS

True to his personality, Ivan tried to win the friendship of other countries before attacking Poland. His hand of friendship was extended to members of the Holy Roman Empire, Hungary, Moldavia, Denmark, and Turkey. He even made an alliance with the Crimean Tatars. Some nations accepted his bid, while others stepped aside but stayed neutral. For the most part Ivan made sure that the war was limited and spread out over a period of many years. It was continued even after Ivan's death by his son, Basil III.

Ivan III was so anxious to spread the Russian border to the west and gain greater power for himself and his homeland that he resorted to methods beyond treaties and warfare. He imprisoned or executed anyone suspected of treason. He took over land belonging to his brothers and was willing to fight them over the rights of ownership.

As history turns out, Ivan's actions were not nearly as severe or terrible as some of the deeds and exploits of his own grandson, Ivan IV, known as Ivan the Terrible.

IVAN THE TERRIBLE

Ivan the Terrible was born in 1530, the son of Basil III, the grand prince of Moscow. By the time he was eight years old, both his parents had died. When Ivan was thirteen, he decided to start his rule by executing his adviser, whom he disliked. This was the beginning of a long series of executions that were to continue throughout his reign. Ivan's favorite way of getting rid of an enemy was to severely torture him, then have him beheaded. Hundreds were killed in that way.

Ilya Repin's painting, Ivan the Terrible and His Son, *shows Ivan cradling his dead son.*

Ivan had difficulty controlling his temper. Once in a fit of rage he struck his favorite son on the head with an iron staff, killing him instantly. His temper led to terrorism. His black-robed private security force, called the oprichniks, roamed the country on black horses. They kept the country clean of traitors. They frightened, plundered, and killed anyone they cared to.

When Ivan decided to marry at age sixteen, he chose Anastasia Zakharina, who belonged to one of the largest of the old Moscow boyar families that did not possess a princely title. She was probably the only person who had any influence over him and for whom he could show any love.

THE FIRST RUSSIAN TSAR

During Ivan's reign as the first tsar of Russia, scholars and artisans were brought from the West to upgrade the Russian civilization. A northern trade route with England was opened.

Left: Tsar Ivan the Terrible, painted by V. Vasnetsov. Right: The tallest bell tower in the Moscow Kremlin is the bell tower of Ivan III.

Diplomacy with European nations and Turkey improved. Russians expanded southward and westward. Trade with the countries in those regions became important. And finally, the great movement eastward into Siberia began. On the military fronts there were some successes in raids into Lithuania and Poland. Border lands in those areas were transferred to Ivan and the Russians.

But inside Russia the extension of serfdom was taking place. The serf's attachment to the soil was tightened, and his freedom to move about or improve his status was further restricted.

Ivan and the other rulers of Russia during the medieval period fought many wars. They helped end outside control and threats to Russia's development as a sovereign nation. These wars increased Russian territories, but wore out the country and made the condition of the peasants worse. It is not clear if these makers of Russian history should be judged as villains or heroes or both.

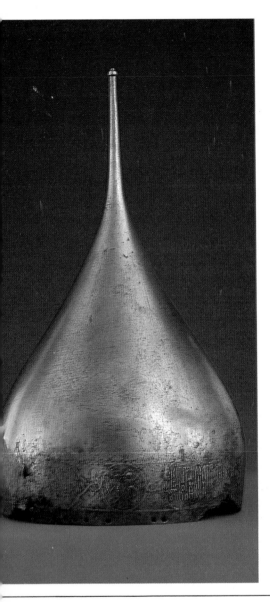
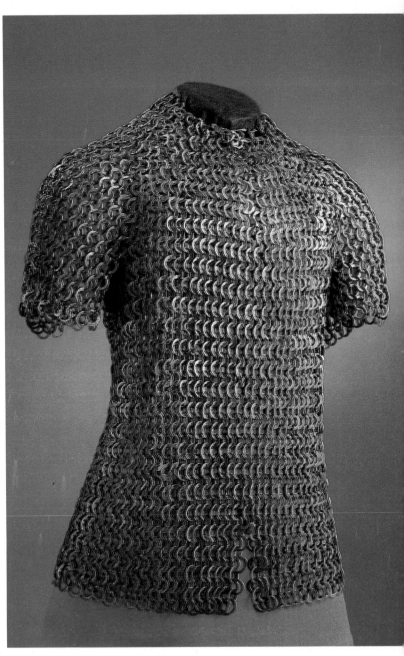

Left: Steel helmet that belonged to the son of Ivan the Terrible.
Right: A coat of chain mail made of large, flat, iron rings that belonged to Boris Godunov.

Chapter 7

RUSSIA'S TIME OF TROUBLES

After Ivan the Terrible died in 1584, a "Time of Troubles" came to Russia. Ivan's death brought on almost thirty years of general confusion, terror, and disregard of laws. People had little use for the weak government. There was utter confusion and disorder.

The unrest in Russia brought on a civil war. Famine across the land caused looting and rioting. Violence and destruction were everywhere. Fearful people accepted rumors as facts. Hardly anyone could be trusted. Spying, plotting, and murder were not uncommon. Roving bands of cossacks, serfs, peasants, and soldiers tried to take matters into their own hands. To add to all these desperate troubles, battles were being fought against the Poles and the Swedes for control of the Russian borders in the west. A tremendous tragedy was taking place in the land of the tsars.

BORIS GODUNOV

Russia needed a very strong ruler at this time. It was unfortunate that Ivan's son Fedor became the tsar. He was a weak-minded, religious young man who his father said was more fit to be a bell ringer in a convent than a tsar. Since Tsar Fedor was unable to rule, the actual power fell to his brother-in-law, the boyar Boris Godunov.

Then Russia's history began to develop like a mystery story, with events so confusing that they remain unsolved to this day. It had started when Ivan's seventh wife gave birth to a son, Dmitry. He might have become tsar when Fedor died, but he was found dead in 1591. Soon it was rumored that Boris had had him murdered to make sure no one would stand in his way of getting possession of the throne.

When Fedor died in 1598, Boris, a very able, rich, and clever man, managed to be "elected" tsar by a popular assembly. For seven hundred years Russia had been ruled by descendants of Rurik. Since Boris was not a blood relative of the previous tsar's family, many were unhappy that he was on the throne and felt that he didn't belong there. Aware of this, Boris put down his opponents, many of them ambitious boyars. He sent them and their families to exile in the distant villages of Siberia.

THE FALSE DMITRY

Then suddenly rumors spread that Dmitry was still alive, that he had miraculously escaped assassination, and that he was living in Poland. The word spread that another child had been buried in his place. Russians believed the news about this "Dmitry" because they wanted a new tsar who would help them with their many troubles.

The Poles accepted the claims of the false Dmitry and used him to gain the support of countless Russians wanting a change. With the help of runaway serfs and brigades of cossacks, always anxious for a reason to go to war for the sake of robbing, the Poles invaded Russia. With this mixed Russian-Polish army, Dmitry's forces arrived at the outskirts of Moscow. Then in 1605, in the middle of war, Tsar Boris died suddenly.

The imposter Dmitry entered Moscow with large units of Polish troops. The Russians thought that Boris's death was his punishment from God, yet they were unwilling to put up with Polish noblemen and their Catholic religion. When the Russians discovered that Dmitry had become a Catholic, they began to reject him as their ruler. His reign lasted less than a year. He was killed in an outbreak started by the boyars, led by Basil Shuisky, a prince. It was said that the false Dmitry was hacked to death, cremated, and his ashes were shot out of a cannon toward Poland.

BASIL IV

Shuisky, backed by the boyars, was placed on the throne as Basil IV. But he was a weak and unreliable ruler. Russia needed a firm hand to stop the bloodshed among the classes and between Russia and foreign armies, mainly the Poles and the Swedes. Bitter fighting continued. The landowners strengthened their powers against the peasants and the peasants joined forces to revolt against them. Armies marched everywhere, some for causes and others merely part of a mob on the move.

THE NEW DMITRY

Russia was still without a strong ruler when, in 1608, another pretender stepped forward. He announced himself as the real

Dmitry, although many knew of his background as a thief and faker. People were so confused and desperate that they seemed willing to accept an imposter as their ruler. When they talked about him they even referred to him as "the thief." Even Marina the beautiful young widow of the first pretender, agreed to accept him as her husband. With the backing of Polish and cossack forces, as well as rebel peasant squads, the new Dmitry set up a second government in an armed camp just outside Moscow. All the while Shuisky tried in vain to rule from the Kremlin. But he acted more like a prisoner than a prince. Life became more unruly in Moscow and troubles mounted.

The worst was still to come. The Poles moved into the fortress of Smolensk and advanced toward Moscow. The Swedes took over Novgorod, still an important trading center for furs and foreign goods. Russia was weakened by feuding and fighting in a land where both the farms and the government were barely operating. Chaos continued and the revolt spread even wider. The "boyar-tsar" Shuisky was dethroned by his own friends. His enemy, the new Dmitry, met a more drastic fate. In the last days of 1610 he was murdered by one of his followers.

EXPELLING THE POLES

The Russian people, tired of the troubles, began to spring back. Their underlying loyalty to "Mother Russia" and the Orthodox church came to the fore. The embarrassment of having a Polish garrison in Moscow triggered the will of the people.

Soon a well-equipped army was trained and organized under Prince Dmitry Pozharsky. Many cossacks volunteered.

By the end of 1612 Moscow and the Kremlin were retaken

An old peasant house

under the able leadership of Prince Pozharsky. Patriotism had prevailed. Moscow was freed. The Poles were defeated, but the bitter feelings between the Russians and the Poles remained.

THE ROMANOVS

The victory of the national army and the reestablishment of rule by Russians made it necessary to choose a new tsar. After much debate sixteen-year-old Mikhail Romanov was selected. The Romanovs were considered one of the great families of Moscow. Mikhail's father was highly respected as the patriarch of Moscow and had many loyal followers. Since Mikhail was so young, his father helped him rule in the early years of his reign. This gave Russia badly needed stability and a tsar young enough to rule for years to come. Mikhail took control of the government of Russia in 1613. With him began the long dynasty of the Romanovs, which was to last until 1917.

*A gold chalice with precious stones was
given to the Cathedral of the Archangel Michael in 1598.*

Chapter 8

NEW BELIEFS
AND "OLD BELIEVERS"

After the "Time of Troubles," the Russian people were faced with the task of starting over. Conditions had to be changed. Improvements and new ideas were needed. Russia had fallen behind the rest of Europe. The national treasury was almost empty. Men would have to exchange weapons for plows if food were to be grown once more. Trade and commerce had to be restored. The government had to be reorganized. Full peace with Poland and Sweden still was not within reach.

In order to raise money to operate the government, taxes were increased greatly. But once again dishonest tax collectors pocketed large sums for themselves. Much of the country's wealth found its way into palaces and churches in the form of gold and jewels. To upgrade the army money had to be given to the generals instead of being used to start new factories or improve farms. Those industries that were started during the 1600s developed with the help of engineers and industrial experts from foreign nations. Foreigners also helped Russia to renew her trade with Holland, England, and Germany.

A NEW CODE OF LAWS

New laws to reorganize the country and strengthen the authority of the tsars were handed down in 1649. The new code of laws again put the central government in a strong position above the lowly peasants. It was declared that the tsar had a God-given "divine" right to rule. Landowners followed the orders of their leader in enforcing the laws. The agricultural workers were once more enslaved and thought of as pieces of property.

RELIGIOUS TROUBLES

At this time an interest developed in changing certain laws and practices of the Russian church as well. The church had become a close partner of the tsarist governments. It did little to speak out against the treatment of the poor or to try to improve their way of life. The clergy were more concerned with details of religious services and ceremonies and the correct wording in prayer books.

Nikon, the patriarch in 1652, wanted to reform the church by taking on many of the rituals of the Greek branch of the Orthodox church. The archpriest Avvakum and his followers, known as "Old Believers," opposed him. They had bitter debates. The religious questions spread to all classes of the population. Although Tsar Alexis privately sided with Nikon's attempts at reform, he failed to support him in public.

Eventually Nikon gave up his position as patriarch of the church and retired to a monastery. Later he went into exile.

Avvakum kept up the fight for his cause, but he was exiled and later was burned at the stake.

Chapter 9

THE RUSSIAN SERFS

Most of the people in Russia from the Middle Ages until 1917 were peasant farmers. During much of this period they were bound to the soil and required to provide large payments and long hours of service to a master. They were known as serfs. The word *serf* comes from the Latin word *servus,* which means slave. But they were not really slaves, nor were they free men.

The expansion of the state of Muscovy in the fifteenth and sixteenth centuries led to an increase in taxation to pay for the many wars and demands of the Russian rulers. Grains needed to be grown in increasing amounts to raise money through trade. At the same time, many landlords were rewarded with large estates for being loyal to the tsar or the nobles. The landlords insisted that the peasants living on their fiefs (feudal estates) pay higher rents and provide longer hours of service. They became lords (of the land) and masters of the peasants, who were being forced deeper and deeper into debt.

A serf's holdings usually included a small log house or a hut, a

Left: Embroidery from the seventeenth century showing the assassination of Prince Dmitry. Right: The Moscow Kremlin is built on the banks of the Moskva River

narrow strip of land, and a few animals. The serf got very little from his field patch. The landlord took most of the peasant's crop as rent payment and as part of his taxes. The serf knew that if he did not pay these taxes promptly he would be severely beaten with a special whip of leather twisted over heavy wire.

For hundreds of years the plight of the peasant serf in Russia was miserable. But not all serfs were willing to accept oppression without doing something about it. Some fled to the frontiers, where life was free but often without law and order. Some left one master and offered themselves to another, hoping to find him less cruel. Serfs were known to join the cossack (free horseman) forces. Many risked their lives by trying to escape to the forestlands of Siberia. Some found their way into large Russian towns and became factory serfs. Those who were caught after leaving their masters without permission were brutally punished or even put to death.

A painting showing the oath of the Don cossacks

REVOLTS AGAINST THE LORDS

Not surprisingly, there was a series of serf revolts against their oppressors. Some of the revolts were small and confined to one area. This happened many times in the seventeenth century. The rebellions were savage. Noblemen were hanged, burned, beaten, whipped, and torn limb from limb. This time it was the peasants who turned violent. The countryside was taken over by roving bands of bandits.

One of the most daring of all the rebel leaders was a bloodthirsty and barbarous Don cossack named Stepan Razin. (Don cossacks were named for the river Don, near which they lived.) This adventurer was a pirate of the Volga River and a raider of rich Persian settlements along the Caspian Sea. He became a legend to thousands of restless cossack horesmen and peasants. In the year 1670 he and his army stirred the imagination of the masses by proclaiming freedom throughout the land. They joined him in a full-fledged peasant war against the tsar and the nobility. Many members of the upper classes were massacred.

Left: Yemelyan Pugachov. Middle: Stepan Razin
Right: Clothing worn during the eighteenth century

Razin's group grew to about 200,000 men. The tsar sent powerful troops south to rout Razin, which they did, but only with great difficulty. The rebellion of Stepan Razin might have been more successful had he not been betrayed by the chief of the Don cossacks whom he had trusted. Razin was taken to Moscow, where he suffered great torture and eventually was executed. He was put to death in 1671 in the square in front of the Kremlin.

PUGACHOV'S REVOLT

The embers of revolt continued to burn for one hundred years after the first large-scale peasant war against serfdom and tsardom. It was during the reign of Empress Catherine II that serfdom reached new heights. She donated over 800,000 serfs to various noblemen as rewards for loyalty and favors. Serf girls were sold for ten rubles, and one noble lady in a course of ten years had 140 serfs, mostly women and girls, tortured to death.

In 1773 another Don cossack soldier, Yemelyan Pugachov, gathered a large army of runaway peasants, serfs from mines and factories, army deserters, religious dissenters, and a variety of minority people and began to capture fortified outposts along the Volga River. Pugachov, too, urged the oppressed people in Russia to join in a fight against their overlords. He promised to end serfdom forever.

Though illiterate, he declared himself to be Emperor Peter III, Catherine's husband, who it was thought had disappeared, but actually had been murdered. He then set out for Moscow, slaughtering noblemen, landowners, officials, merchants, and priests along the way. Catherine was forced to send her best troops against Pugachov in the summer of 1774. The rebel army proved to be no match against highly trained troops. With the civil war spreading and the peasants away from the farms, the land was being neglected. Famine was everywhere. Only Catherine's soldiers and favored noblemen seemed to have enough food. With Pugachov's army starving, some loyal cossacks, more concerned about their own lives than their struggle, surrendered their tired leader to the Russian army. Pugachov was taken to Moscow in a wooden cage and put to death on January 10, 1775.

The landowners returned to their lands more powerful than ever. The serfs were forced back to their lowly status with conditions worse than before the revolt. The rebellions, though unsuccessful in doing away with serfdom, convinced the serfs that they would have to continue their fight for freedom.

The "Cap of Monomach" from the minor robes of state of Peter the Great. The cap is gold, decorated with precious stones and pearls, and edged with sable.

Chapter 10

PETER THE GREAT

Peter I, tsar of Russia, stood more than 6 feet, 6 inches (2 meters, 152 millimeters) in his stocking feet. When he put on his high boots he measured nearly 7 feet (over 2 meters) tall. He was muscular and strong; during his forty-three-year reign as tsar and emperor he helped make his country muscular and strong as well. While he ruled, Russia became a great empire. This is why he was called Peter the Great.

Because of Peter's deep desire to have Russia recognized as a powerful country, he set out to learn about the successes of other European nations. He personally went abroad to study their way of life. He liked what he saw and was determined to modernize Russia. He returned home ready to build "a window to Europe." *1703* He built a new city near the Baltic Sea, a city of stone, not of wood like the old Russian cities, and named it St. Petersburg.

PETER'S YOUTH

Peter's early life had a major influence on his ideas and deeds as tsar. When his father Alexis died in 1676, Peter was only four years old. He received very little formal education despite the fact that he was curious and quite bright. He worked hard at everything he undertook, be it carpentry, cabinetwork, printing, sailing, or blacksmithing. He bragged that he had mastered fifteen trades, including dentistry. He had a passion to perform well and to be as practical as possible.

Peter had good hands for making his own top boots and for mending his clothes. He disliked the oriental type of robes (caftans) worn by old-fashioned boyars. He also hated the long beards that most Russian men grew. When he became tsar he ordered both beards and long robes cut. On a few occasions Peter personally took shears in hand and trimmed the beards and caftans of some of his chief boyars. Only those who paid a special beard tax in Russia were allowed to grow long hair on their faces. Beards were tax-free to peasants. Peter realized that upper-class men would not want to be mistaken for lowly peasants.

As a practical young man Peter decided to go overseas, mostly to learn how to build ships. He was the first tsar ever to leave Moscow. Although he tried to hide his identity, he was often recognized because of his size. He worked as a ship's carpenter in Holland and then went to Great Britain, where he also worked in shipyards. While in Europe he hired over one thousand experts to take their skills to Russia.

TSAR PETER

Peter the Great went to extremes to do away with anyone, anything, or any country that prevented Russia from coming out of the dark ages to join more modern nations. He believed that he was appointed by God to accomplish that task. It had been his dream even before he became sole tsar of Russia at age twenty-

Left: A painting showing the morning of the streltsy execution, by V. Surikov
Right: Peter the Great's portrait hangs in the Tsar's Summer Palace at Pushkino on the outskirts of St. Petersburg, now Leningrad.

four. Before then he shared the throne with a sickly and weak-minded older brother, Ivan V.

The actual ruling was done by Peter's older half sister, Sophia, who was made regent (a person chosen to rule while a king is sick or too young). Sophia proved to be ambitious, clever, and well meaning. She also meant to keep Peter from getting the throne. This led to a struggle for power by groups of relatives and others trying to control the throne for Ivan or Sophia. The plotting and fighting by those close to the palace, including a revolt by the streltsy (the tsar's personal bodyguards), caused unrest and bloodshed in the Kremlin. When the army took the side of Peter against those supporting his half sister, Peter was able to win the throne. As tsar, he had Sophia placed in a convent, where she became a nun. The streltsy were brutally executed.

Safely in power, Tsar Peter began to war against Russia's neighbors to the south and north. He declared war on Turkey in 1695 in order to gain an outlet to the Black Sea and end Russia's being landlocked in the south. At first Peter's campaign was a failure and he was unable to take Azov, the Turkish fortress on the Sea of Azov in the Crimea. With his background in sailing and shipbuilding he quickly built a fleet, sailed down the Don River, and cut off Turkey's garrison at Azov from the sea-lanes to Constantinople. Within a year Azov surrendered and Peter made up his mind to build a bigger and better navy—even if he had to go to the countries that knew how to build the best ships.

WAR WITH SWEDEN

Peter gave up his plans to win control of the Black Sea and turned his attention to the Baltic seacoast instead. But the Swedish king, Charles XII, had spies in Russia and knew of Peter's plans. He rushed soldiers to the region and blocked Russia's way to the Baltic coast. That did not block Peter's strong determination to continue the fight against his young opponent. Charles XII was barely eighteen years old at the time, but was very daring and able as a military leader. The Northern War started in 1700 and lasted for twenty-one years. Peter made alliances with friendly countries, worked out treaties, and took complete charge of the army and navy. Not only did Peter lay out the strategy of the military campaigns, but he personally fought as an officer on the battlefield and as a sailor on the deck of a warship. He even worked as a laborer in Russian shipyards, doing all he could to speed up the production of naval vessels.

Since King Charles XII led the strongest army in Europe, Tsar

RUSSIA IN 1689
—— Russia's Border Today

Peter the Great at Poltava

Peter's armies suffered some early defeats, until the Battle of Poltava in 1709. There Peter thought of a way to divide and weaken the powerful Swedish army, which always had had great success in attacking the main fortress of an enemy. He had his engineers build a series of small forts away from the main fort, positioning them in the path of the Swedish army. Thus he was able to split their forces into little groups and prevent a single, fierce attack. Peter also supervised and fought in the naval battle of Gangut in 1714, which turned out to be Russia's first victory at sea.

WAR ON TWO FRONTS

While the war with Sweden continued, fighting also started again with Turkey. The Turkish War lasted from 1710 to 1713. Peter had to divide his army and fight a two-front war. His weakened army to the south was surrounded by much larger

Turkish forces on the Prut River. Peter learned that it was better to fight one enemy at a time, so he signed a treaty of peace with Turkey and returned Azov to them. From that time on his military effort was concentrated on winning the war against Sweden. This was accomplished by 1721. Sweden became a lesser power, the eastern shores of the Baltic Sea came under Russian control, and Russia's archenemy Poland came under Russian domination. With the war in the north completed, Peter was now free to wage a successful campaign against Persia in 1722/23. At last the Russian flag flew over the shores of the Caspian Sea. Peter was so delighted with his victories and the expansion of Russian territories that he celebrated by changing his title from tsar to emperor of all the Russias.

PETER'S SON ALEXIS

Leaders like Peter the Great come to realize that along with military victories there must also be defeats. Yet, Peter always seemed to learn from his defeats by turning them into victories. He profited from his mistakes by not repeating them. He seemed able to overcome most disappointments, except one—that was his unhappiness with his son Alexis, the natural heir to the throne. Alexis did not measure up to his father's expectations. He did not have Peter's firm autocratic manner, strength, capacity for long hours of work, courage, or intelligence.

The clergy and other people around Alexis tried to influence him to return Russia to her old non-Western ways should he become tsar. Peter was worried that when he died his peace-loving son would stop the building of St. Petersburg, a Western-type city, abolish the fleet, and reduce the size of the army.

Peter the Great's throne room (left) and his parade carriage (right) can be seen in the Hermitage Museum in Leningrad.

Peter not only disliked Alexis, he distrusted him as well. He knew that many of his enemies hoped that Alexis would soon become tsar, even if it meant that Peter would have to be overthrown or killed. Though Alexis wished for his father's death, he had not planned to bring it about. Feeling guilty because of these wicked thoughts, he decided to give up his rights to the throne and he fled to Austria. Peter feared that Alexis would remain there until after his father's death, then claim his right to be tsar and undo everything Peter had done for Russia, the country he loved so much. He tricked his son into returning home by promising that he would not be harmed.

Once Alexis returned, he was charged with treason, put in a cell, and badly tortured. Sometimes he even was tortured in the presence of his father, who wanted to know which men were using his son to plot against him. Alexis finally died after weeks of torture. Peter cried bitterly at his son's deathbed and at his funeral. Though many of Alexis's friends were also tortured and executed, no proof of a plot against Peter ever was found.

A gold cross, set with precious stones, that belonged to Peter the Great

The tomb of Peter the Great in the Peter and Paul Cathedral in St. Petersburg, now Leningrad. All the Romanovs after Peter the Great were buried here— the oldest church in Leningrad.

THE DEATH OF PETER THE GREAT

In the years after Alexis's death, Peter fought harder, worked harder, and played harder. This put a great strain on his health. He rarely rested. While sailing in the Gulf of Finland, he came upon some Russian soldiers shipwrecked on a sandbank. Peter bravely plunged into the icy waters and rescued several men. He caught pneumonia and died in St. Petersburg, his beloved new city, the mark of his modernization of Russia. He was fifty-three years old.

Peter the Great left an empire, but he left no one to be his successor. His widow, Catherine, became empress and succeeded to his throne. The rulers that followed Peter were weak. During the next thirty-seven years Russia experienced five palace revolutions. The empire began to decline—until another Catherine, the widow of the murdered Tsar Peter III, came to power. And she became known as Catherine the Great.

*Left: A portrait of
Catherine the Great
Below: The Winter Palace
(now called the Hermitage)
is now an art museum.
During her reign Catherine the Great
began buying some of
the paintings now found here.*

Chapter 11

CATHERINE THE GREAT

Peter the Great had looked to the countries of western Europe for help in making Russia a powerful state. Little did he imagine that upon his very throne eventually would sit an import from one of those nations, a German princess then named Sophia but later called Catherine. She ruled Russia at the end of the eighteenth century, from 1762 to 1796.

CATHERINE'S UNHAPPY MARRIAGE

When Catherine was fifteen years old, it was arranged for her to be taken to Russia to marry Grand Duke Peter (later Peter III), heir to the Russian throne. Her father, a German prince, and Frederick the Great of Prussia thought her marriage to a Russian would strengthen the friendship of the two countries. It also would weaken the influence in Russia of Austria, Prussia's enemy.

Had Catherine known in advance what the grand duke was like, she probably would never have left home. Peter would not have been a good husband for any girl, let alone one as pretty, charming, intelligent, and full of energy as Catherine. Her husband was weak, undersized, and certainly far from being handsome. His mind was subnormal and Catherine thought he was an idiot, especially when he turned cruel. Though she had very little to do with him, she outwardly remained married. As a very ambitious young lady, she knew that as the grand duchess she would sooner or later rise to power.

Catherine and Peter had strange relationships with one another and with the Russian nobility. Peter was unpopular. He was born and raised in a German duchy in Denmark and did not speak Russian well. She, on the other hand, though of German birth, took on many of the Russian ways and became popular and admired, especially by many of the palace agents and ministers. Many Russians, and others throughout Europe, felt that she was too close to her advisers, completely overlooking her husband. There was considerable gossip about her behavior. Yet, Catherine did not divorce Peter. Apparently she had other plans.

TSARINA CATHERINE

When Peter's aunt, the Empress Elizabeth, died in 1762, he succeeded her on the throne, but his stay there was short. In six months one of Catherine's best friends, Grigori Orlov, and his brother Aleksei, with the help of the Imperial Guards, forced Peter to give up his right to rule. Catherine was rushed to St. Petersburg and proclaimed empress of Russia. Since few people respected Peter, his overthrow was readily accepted. Eight days later Peter was murdered at his country home, probably by Aleksei Orlov, but that, too, was accepted.

At age thirty-three Catherine was crowned autocrat, a ruler with unlimited power, and for the next thirty-four years that is

A section of the ceiling in the Winter Palace, now the Hermitage

exactly how she reigned. Though her private life was scandalous, with at least twenty male companions, she never permitted her personal associations to interfere with her conduct of state affairs. She was too vain to allow anyone else to govern Russia, not even the favorite men she fell in love with.

Catherine's main interests were intellectual and political. Under her leadership the empire continued to expand. There was little change within the country, however, for Catherine wanted to be well liked by the nobles who had allowed her to become tsarina. Catherine enjoyed reading the latest books written by such great original thinkers as Voltaire and Diderot, who called for governments to grant freedom and equality. She even corresponded with these brilliant men and other famous authors and statesmen. Some of these outstanding men of letters came to Russia as Catherine's guests and found her conversations to be witty and interesting. She was most concerned about the high standards of manners used in the social circles of Paris and Berlin. She wanted that kind of culture for Russian society as well.

An icon, showing three female saints, painted during the eighteenth century

EDUCATION AND THE ARTS

In 1764 Catherine founded the first school for girls in St. Petersburg. She encouraged writers and scientists, especially doctors and surgeons, to visit Russia and share their knowledge. She set a brave example by her willingness to take a smallpox inoculation, which was just being introduced in Russia. Catherine built foundling homes for young children deserted by their parents, a public library, a medical college and town clinics, and the Winter Palace—now called the Hermitage—one of Russia's chief art museums.

Prince Gregory Potemkin, one of Catherine the Great's favorites

CATHERINE'S FAVORITES

Catherine conducted her own foreign policy. Though she listened to her generals and diplomats, she usually made the final decisions in gaining more territory for Russia. She respected the military achievements of Alexander Suvorov, one of Russia's greatest generals, who defeated the Turks and Poles on two separate fronts in the south and west.

Catherine was especially fond of Prince Gregory Potemkin. As one of the Imperial Guards he had an important role in putting Catherine on the throne. Potemkin appealed to Catherine with his great size, energy, and sense of humor. He was fun to be with and when he imitated the palace notables Catherine would laugh uproariously. Potemkin could even get away with making fun of the tsarina's German accent. He was so much in her favor that she allowed him to plan and conduct the successful war against Turkey when much of southern Russia and the Crimea were conquered. Catherine was so pleased with Potemkin that she made him a prince of that region and built for him a fantastic palace where the greatest parties in all of Europe were held.

The poor people of Russia became bitter when they learned of these lavish affairs. Some were able to see firsthand how grand the empress was treated when they flocked along the route of her famous journey in 1787 to inspect new possessions in the Ukraine and the Crimea.

The expedition was arranged by Potemkin. Catherine traveled over ice and snow in an enclosed sleigh consisting of several rooms pulled by thirty horses. Supplies and attendants traveled along in 150 additional sleighs. When spring arrived and the ice broke at the city of Kiev, the entire party sailed down the Dnieper River. The parade of boats was led by seven enormous houseboats, each painted red and gold, followed by seventy-three smaller support boats manned by three thousand sailors. At night Catherine would stay at nobles' homes along the shores. If none were available, Potemkin would have one quickly built for his empress's comfort.

THE DEATH OF CATHERINE THE GREAT

Catherine the Great never got as far as Constantinople, even though Potemkin surprised her by placing a huge signpost enroute reading "To Constantinople." Though it was her ambition to conquer Turkey and control all of the Black Sea, she never reached that objective. Catherine died of a stroke in 1796. She was able to win large parts of Poland, however, and in two wars against Turkey the Crimea came under Russian control. Russian ships were able to gain free access to the Black Sea.

Chapter 12

TSAR PAUL,
TSAR ALEXANDER,
AND NAPOLEON

During the late 1700s and the first decades of the 1800s, trouble in western Europe threatened to spread eastward. The French emperor Napoleon had seized many countries on the continent and was turning toward Russia. The revolution in France, with the creation in 1792 of the first French republic and the overthrow of the monarchy, was beginning to catch on elsewhere as well. Rulers of countries were being murdered, executed, or exiled. The lower classes were rioting for their rights. Philosophers and writers were spreading ideas of freedom and equality. England and France were struggling for a colonial empire.

The Russian tsars were afraid these problems would affect the people of their country—and that is what happened.

TSAR PAUL

Russia became a major power after Catherine. She was succeeded by her son Paul, who, like Ivan the Terrible and Peter the Great, was very temperamental, if not a little insane. Many referred to Paul as the "Mad Tsar." Paul was embittered at being blocked from becoming tsar thirty-four years earlier by his

MURMANSK • Pustozersk

NORWAY SWEDEN LAPPS SAMOEDS OSTIA

White Sea Usf-Tsilma *Pechora* URAL

FINLAND *To Sweden 1617* *To Russia 1721* *Mezen* *N. Dvina*

Arkhangelsk Denisovka *Vychegda* Ust-Vym

Kholmogory Sol-Vychegodsk Cherdyn

Abo *Lake Onega* Velikii Ustiug *Iug* Solikamsk

Viborg Petrozavodsk *Sukhona*

Helsinki Belozersk *Unzha* Viatka Perm

Stockholm DAGO Reval St. Petersburg *To Sweden 1617* *To Russia 1721* Vologda *M O U N T A I N S*

GOTLAND *To Russia 1721* Kronstadt Belozersk

ESTHONIA Novgorod Kostroma

OSEL *Gulf of Riga* *Lake Peipus* Pskov *Lake Ilmen* CHERMISSIANS

To Russia 1721 LIVONIA Libau Riga *W. Dvina* Velikie Luki Tver Vladimir Nizhni-Novgorod

Memel LITHUANIA Polotsk Rzhev *Volga* Kazan Ufa

Danzig Königsberg Kovno Vitebsk *Dnieper* Viazma Moscow Arzamas BASHKI

Thorn EAST PRUSSIA Grodno Vilno *To Russia 1772, 1793, 1795* Orsha Smolensk Kaluga *Oka* Riazan Temnikov Simbirsk *To Russia in 17th Century*

Minsk Mogilev Briansk Tula Orel MORDVIANS Penza Samara

Warsaw Slonim *Bug* *Dnieper* Viazma Orel Tambov Saratov Orenburg

Brest-Litovsk Pinsk *Pripet* Kursk *Don* *Khoper* *To Russia 1734*

POLAND Lublin Mozyr Gomel *Desna* Voronezh *Medveditsa* Uralsk *Ural (Jaik)* *To Russia 1731-1824*

Krakow *To Russia 1772, 1793, 1795* Chernigov Belgorod *Volga* Tsaritsyn

Republic of Krakow 1815-1846 *To Austria 1846* Lvov Zhitomir Kiev *To Russia 1654-1686* Kharkov DON COSSACKS Gurev

GALICIA Tarnopol UKRAINE Cherkassy Poltava *Donets* *To Russia 1696-1711 1733-1739*

Kamenets-Podolsk Chotin Uman Elizavetgrad *S. Bug* Ekaterinoslav *To Russia 1733-1739* Novocherkassk KALMUKS TATARS

Budapest BUKO BESSARABIA Jassy Kishinev *To Russia 1791* Novai Sech ZAPOROZHIE Novocherkassk Rostov Astrakhan

HUNGARY Kamenets VINA Bender Ochakov *To Russia 1783* Taganrog Azov *Don*

TRANSYLVANIA MOLDAVIA Odessa *To Russia 1774* Kherson *Sea of Azov* *To Russia 1783*

To Moldavia 1856-1878 Akkerman Kinburin Perekop *To Russia 1812* *Kuban* Stavropol Fort Aleksandrovskii *To Russia 1723-1732*

WALLACHIA Ismail *To Russia 1878* CRIMEA Kerch Ekaterinodar CIRCASSIA *To Russia 1761-1825* Tarki *To Russia 1723-1732*

To Rumania 1878 *To Russia 1829* *To Turkey 1856-78* Simferopol Anapa Novorossiisk Mozdok *Terek* Derbent *1830*

Bucharest Sevastopol Sinope Piatigorsk Vladikavkaz DAGHESTAN

BALKAN MTS. Ruschuk Kuchuk-Kainardji *Black Sea* Sukhum-Kale MINGRELIA GEORGIA Shemakha *To Russia 1723-1732*

BULGARIA *To Rumania 1878* *Danube* Poti Kutaisi Tiflis *To Russia 1801* Elizavetpol Baku

SERBIA Sinope Batum Ardahan KARABAKH *1804-1813* *To Russia 1813*

Trebizond *To Russia 1878* Kars Erivan *To Russia 1828* Lenkoran Astara

ARMENIA Erzerum Lake Van *Araks* Tabriz

© Rand McNally & Co., R.L. 83-5-46

EXPANSION OF RUSSIA IN EUROPE

MILES 0 50 100 200 300 400

Russia 1533

Acquired to 1914

Acquired to 1598

Held at other times

Dates indicate time area held or gained by Russia.

mother and her close friends. He hated them for that and carried a grudge against them all his life.

When Catherine died, Paul ordered the remains of his father, Tsar Peter III, buried for thirty-four years, dug up and placed in a coffin. The suspected murderer, Alekesi Orlov, was made to walk in a procession behind the body, carrying the former tsar's crown to the cathedral. There Catherine and her long-dead husband were displayed side by side. Those friends of his mother who were still alive were made to stand guard over the pair, for all to see. It was a shocking scene, but in his way Paul got his revenge. He didn't stop with that, either. Potemkin's corpse was taken from its elaborate burial place and dumped in a pit.

PAUL'S REFORMS

Not everything Paul did as tsar verged on the insane. He brought back the law of primogeniture. This meant that only the firstborn had the right to inherit the crown. He remodeled the army and navy after the Prussian military forces. While Paul made some attempts at improving the life of the serfs, he also forced many peasants into serfdom. Education and commerce were improved. During Paul's reign of less than six years the

Russian army, once more under the brilliant leadership of General Suvorov, gained impressive victories in campaigns that took his troops across half of Europe, all the way to northern Italy. Russia was now considered a major power and other nations sought her friendship. England and France were at odds with each other and Russia would side with one or the other, depending on which country could better help her interests.

As Paul concerned himself about the possibilities of advances on Russia from foreign enemies, he also feared his own destruction from within the country. On the night of March 23, 1801, Tsar Paul was betrayed by the men around him and by his trusted Imperial Guards. Assassins broke into his bedroom and butchered him.

TSAR ALEXANDER I

Alexander I ruled Russia for almost a quarter of a century from 1801 to 1825. Alexander spoke excellent English and French, which he knew better than Russian. Thus he could deal directly with the foreign ministers of England and France. He had to decide whether to enter into an alliance with one or the other. When he met Napoleon, the emperor of France, it was obvious they disliked each other. There was much competition as to who would eventually reign supreme on the European continent.

For a number of years Alexander was advised by one of Russia's most able and interesting statesmen, Mikhail Speransky. He wanted Russia to have a constitution that would give greater rights to more Russians through their own legislatures, which were to be elected by nobles and free peasants. There would be basic laws that everyone would have to obey. At first he was able to convince Alexander to abolish torture and the selling of serfs. It was his idea that Russia could continue its monarchy, but with the powers of government separated. In his own mind he hoped that serfdom would be done away with. The powerful nobles around Alexander persuaded the tsar not to listen to Speransky. In 1812 Speransky was dismissed and exiled for many years. Those opposed to him said his reforms were like the new ideas coming out of France and would not be good for Russia.

NAPOLEON BONAPARTE

More than ideas were coming out of France at this time. Napoleon Bonaparte and his great armies were on the move. Very ambitious, he wasn't satisfied merely being emperor of France. He was eyeing the rest of Europe, especially Russia. The two countries had differences over trade relations and economic agreements. Russia began to give up on her promises to help blockade England, France's enemy. At times Alexander favored England, but during earlier years he had sided with France. England and Russia managed to carry on trade that was very important for the Russian economy. Napoleon had hoped to get more direct support from Russia, but Alexander always held back. Napoleon conquered Italy, Germany, and Spain, and Russia was beginning to feel threatened. Alexander knew that he couldn't trust Napoleon. He was right, for in 1812 Napoleon led an army three times as large as Russia's onto Russian soil.

NAPOLEON'S GRAND ARMY

Napoleon's huge invading force of 640,000 men was called the

Grand Army. At first the French won every battle. They were easily able to advance inside Russia, using lightweight pontoon bridges to cross the numerous north-south flowing rivers. The Russians retreated. The commander in chief, old Field Marshal Mikhail Kutuzov, had a clever plan. He would rely on Russian patriotism, time, space, and a Russian secret weapon that Napoleon knew nothing about—the harsh Russian winter. The deeper Napoleon advanced toward Moscow, the longer and thinner became his supply lines. Kutuzov knew that. So he refused to do battle with the French army, choosing to defend his country far from the border, at Borodino, 65 miles (105 kilometers) west of Moscow.

It is estimated that 250,000 soldiers took part in the battle and 1,200 cannon were used by both sides. The Russian soldiers fought with honor and bravery against the experienced but weary French troops. The fighting was fierce. The forces met head on. Both armies lost 40,000 men and several generals. By nightfall the grounds around Borodino were a terrible sight, reddened from the blood of the fallen. Later Napoleon wrote: "Of the fifty battles which I have directed the battle near Moscow was fought with the greatest valor and brought us the least success. . . ."

Until the great Battle of Borodino, most of the generals of Europe did not believe Napoleon's armies could be halted. Many thought he would defeat the Russians without much difficulty and advance all the way to India. Some thought that he was out to conquer the world. Though neither side won a convincing victory at Borodino, the Russians were much too weakened to defend Moscow. They left it to the French, but not before they set fire to the city. It took the French nearly a month to put out all the flames.

The retreat of Napoleon's army

THE FRENCH RETREAT

Alexander, safe in St. Petersburg, refused to surrender to Napoleon. Napoleon's supplies were getting lower and so were the temperatures. The Russian winter had set in; each day the weather got colder and colder. When Napoleon learned that countless numbers of his soldiers were suffering from frostbite, he decided to retreat from Moscow.

The French retreat was one of the most disastrous marches any army has ever made. When the survivors of the French army finally straggled across the frontier into Poland, only 9,000 men remained of the 100,000 that were ordered to abandon Moscow.

Russia gained land, confidence, and prestige throughout Europe after her encounter with Napoleon. Before invading Russia, Napoleon had said: "In three years I will rule the world. . . . Russia remains but I shall crush her. . . . " But there were some things his military maps could not tell him. The great French field commander met his match in the determination of Tsar Alexander, the patience of Field Marshal Kutuzov, the self-sacrifice of the Russian people, and the most formidable enemy of all—the Russian winter!

During the reign of Tsar Nicholas I (above left) many Russians demanded reforms and social justice. The differences between the wealthy and the common man were too great. Above middle: A working man. Above right: Marriage of a wealthy couple. Revolutionaries were watched and some were exiled to Siberia. Below: A prisoner says farewell to his family.

Chapter 13

THE DECEMBRIST REBELS AND TSAR NICHOLAS I

During the years of the Napoleonic wars many young officers of the Russian army serving abroad were able to see firsthand the progress being made by other governments. They observed the prosperity of western Europe. They noted the freedom enjoyed in France and Germany. They admired the educational institutions. In Russia the advancements were few.

The tsar was still ruling with a firm hand. The common man had yet to gain liberty and equality—those ideals seemed only for dreamers. Education was available, but only for the upper classes. The nobles continued to receive special privileges. Justice was uncertain, if not unfair, especially for the lower classes.

TSAR NICHOLAS I

Tsar Alexander had no children. When he died suddenly, there was much confusion as to who would be the new tsar. A brother, Constantine, decided not to accept the throne. For a brief period the throne was unoccupied until Nicholas I was proclaimed tsar.

Colonel Pavel Pestel, the respected poet Kondraty Ryleyev, and other founders of a secret society quickly concluded that this would be a good time to revolt. Their plan envisaged the capture of the Winter Palace and the St. Peter and Paul Fortress in St. Petersburg. They hoped to arrest the royal family and round up the high government ministers.

The plan failed. At the appointed time, on December 14, 1825, the revolutionary officers were able to rally the support of only three thousand rebels. Shots were fired at the government troops loyal to the tsar, but their ranks were not broken. The rebel force was much too weak in number. Their palace-type revolt in St. Petersburg and a simultaneous uprising in the Ukraine were quickly put down. On the order of the new Tsar Nicholas, soldiers opened fire on the rebels and crushed the revolt as thousands gathered nearby to watch. Five hundred of Colonel Pestel's insurgents were killed.

The Decembrist rebels were afraid of a truly popular uprising of the people at this time. They wanted to act "for the people but without the people." It didn't work. But revolutionary shots were fired into the air and they were heard. More than one hundred of the best-educated and idealistic sons of Russia were exiled to Siberia. Pestel, Ryleyev, and three others were hanged. The uprising led by the Decembrists was the first revolutionary movement against tsarism.

UNREST AND DISORDER

For Nicholas the revolution was a warning. He was deeply concerned. While he was tsar, almost five hundred disorders took place, mainly in agricultural districts. Russia was also becoming an industrial country during the thirty years of Nicholas's reign (1825-1855). Factory workers began to show some unrest with a few protests and demands for greater benefits. Nicholas added a new department to the government. Called the Third Department, it was a brutal secret police force that snuffed out subversion and revolution.

Nicholas refused to allow more than three hundred students to attend any university at a time. He placed trusted military men in high government offices. Few Russians were allowed to travel outside the country. Spying was widespread. Liberal nobles were watched. Sometimes the secret police would infiltrate the inner circles of organizations with "plants" who would inform the authorities about their goals and plans. When they were turned in, as thousands were, they were exiled to Siberia. The great Russian novelist Fedor Dostoyevsky was chained and exiled to Siberia because he belonged to a political society the tsar feared.

THE CRIMEAN WAR

Not only did Nicholas want to impose his will on Russia, he also wanted to control events elsewhere. In 1853 he became involved in a war with Turkey, at first over the matter of protection for Orthodox priests, Russian Christians, and holy places in Palestine. Russia had hoped to expand its influence in the Balkans and the Near East. Fearing this, Great Britain, France, and Sardinia came to the aid of the Turks in 1854. Their fleets sailed into the Black Sea and invaded the Crimean Peninsula. The war was fought badly by both sides, but Russian soldiers showed considerable bravery in their defense of the key fortress at Sevastopol. The Russian defeat in the Crimean War was caused

mostly by inferior equipment, failure of the supply system, and costly mistakes made by the corrupt and autocratic bureaucracy in Moscow. The loss showed that Russia was beginning to fall behind the industrial nations of Europe.

THE DEATH OF NICHOLAS

In March of 1855, Nicholas I, exhausted and greatly troubled by the turn of events in the Crimea, died. It is thought that not only did Nicholas foresee the collapse of his military forces in the south, but that he began to realize that his system of authoritarian rule, which he had continued to build in order to save Russia from revolution, would sooner or later also be doomed.

Chapter 14

EXPANSION IN ASIA

After its defeat in the Crimean War, Russia began to expand in Asia. The vast plains of Siberia had been crossed by Russian traders from Novgorod as early as the eleventh century. But the occupation of Siberia was slow. Over the centuries small bands of settlers and cossacks penetrated the steppe lands, taiga (coniferous forest), and marshes of Asia in quest of freedom and adventure. Some had religious motives. Others wanted riches. Most migrated eastward toward the endless horizon following the age-old call of "gospel, gold, and glory."

YERMAK

In 1558 Grigory Stroganov was granted certain privileges to build and operate salt works and start farms in the undeveloped lands in the east. As Stroganov reaped large profits from his grants, he hired a party of Volga cossacks to protect his possessions. One of the cossacks was an adventuresome leader named Yermak (Ermak Timofeyevich), a former robber and pirate once condemned to death for rebellion. In 1581 Yermak led an expedition of eight hundred men east of the Urals by sailing flat-bottom boats up and down the rivers and dragging them between navigable waters. He easily defeated the Tatar armies in his path with firearms and took the city of Sibir, which was later to give its name to the great Siberian region.

Yermak was a clever man. Wisely, he returned to Moscow with his captured booty and shared his prizes with Tsar Ivan IV. He was pardoned for his past misdeeds and crimes and in turn received rich gifts. With Ivan's support Yermak returned to Siberia and penetrated deep into central Asia, where he built little fortresses, called ostrogs, equipped with guns. These garrisons, manned by Yermak's followers, helped defend the newly acquired region for Russia and were the beginnings of today's great cities of Siberia. In 1584 Yermak drowned in a river during a battle.

RUSSIAN EXPLORERS

After Yermak blazed a path into Siberia, a number of other explorers and cossacks continued farther into the interior. Poiarkov reached the Amur River in the Far East in 1644. Semyon Dezhnev, in 1648, took an expedition all the way to Asia's northeastern tip and then steered one of his small sailing vessels into the strait that separates Asia from North America. He discovered the seaway between the Arctic and Pacific oceans. Eighty years later a seafarer named Vitus Bering sailed through the strait and described it for navigators and early mapmakers. Today that strait bears his name.

In 1650 Yerofei Khabarov took his cossacks to the Amur River close to an area that is presently China. In order to reach that distant territory, some of the cossacks had to march along riverbanks pulling their heavily loaded boats against strong currents. During the winter months they were forced to build skis and large sleds for transporting their boats, cannon, and supplies across Asia's high mountains. In 1697 Vladimir Atlasov discovered the Kamchatka, a peninsula that juts out into the northern Pacific for 700 miles (1,126 kilometers).

DISPUTED TERRITORIES

In 1689 a treaty was signed between the Russians and the Chinese over rights to the lands on both sides of the Amur River. This settled the question of Mongolia, which remained under China's influence for many years thereafter. The treaty, signed at Nerchinsk, brought peace to the area for more than 150 years.

As trade with China developed, so did clashes between the cossacks and Chinese armies over disputed territories. In 1858 and 1860, the Chinese signed treaties giving Russia control of the regions north of the Amur River and east of the Ussuri River.

By 1864 Russian troops had wiped out tribes of rebel raiders in the Caucasus Mountains. Most of central Asia was occupied after a series of military campaigns from 1865 to 1876. In order to expand into the southwestern interior of Asia, the Russians had to subdue the Khivans, a determined group of people who had lived for centuries in the dry oases around the Aral Sea. The Khivans had a reputation for ferocious fighting.

Russia's expansion to the east extended beyond Asia into North America, including the territory of Alaska. In 1867 the Russian government sold Alaska to the United States.

Above left: Yermak, one of the pioneers of Siberia. Above right: A log cabin of a Russian settler in western Siberia in 1910

DEVELOPING SIBERIA

The early explorers and colonizers of Siberia were mainly cossack officers, officials from Moscow, monks, and merchants. At first Russian economic activity was limited to collecting tribute from the local or native inhabitants. As agriculture and mining became more important, an increasing number of strong young men ran away from their horrible lives and tried to make their fortunes in Siberia.

Many criminals escaped to the new frontiers in the east. The Russian government began sending convicts to miserable Siberian prison camps where they were forced to work in mines under the watch of brutal guards. Some of these prisoners were allowed to live and work in isolated village outposts. After they served their sentences, many decided to stay on in Siberia.

Above left: The first train on the Transbaikalia Railroad in 1900. Above right: The main street of the Siberian town of Mariinsk in 1898

In the nineteenth century there was no railroad across Siberia. The few roads that were built—often by convicts—were rough and hard to travel. The frozen rivers proved to be much more reliable. To reach their destinations, prisoners were usually chained together and marched for hundreds of miles. Thousands never arrived, dying from starvation, disease, exhaustion, or the cold. Those that went mad or were too weak or sick to march were either shot or left to die alone.

The greatest conquest of Siberia came with the completion of the 5,000-mile (9,332-kilometer) Trans-Siberian Railroad. Started in 1891 and completed in 1905, the single-track line spanned Siberia from Moscow in the west to Vladivostok, the port city on the Pacific. The construction of the railroad brought hundreds of thousands of new colonists to Siberia. They were railway workers, farmers, miners, and other young Russians seeking new opportunities.

Above: The double-headed eagle was a symbol of the tsars.
Left: Tsar Alexander II

Chapter 15

ALEXANDER II, NICHOLAS II, AND THE ROAD TO REVOLUTION

As soon as Alexander II became tsar in 1855, he realized that drastic changes would have to be made in Russia to prevent a revolution or a collapse of the government from within. Russia's defeat in the Crimean War proved that the country was falling behind the rest of the major powers of Europe. Alexander knew that Russia was backward and that her industrial growth was slow. He no longer could hide the fact that in addition to the serfs, many others were beginning to demand reforms and social justice. It seemed everyone was against serfdom.

FREEING THE SERFS

Alexander finally decided to abolish serfdom. Serfs were to be granted their personal liberty, but would not be allowed to leave the land. The landlords would not let their lands be taken away from them and divided into plots for the serfs to farm. Besides, most serfs knew only how to work the land. They did not know how to operate a farm. So Alexander came up with a plan to hand the land over to the serfs gradually. The serfs would be able to purchase the land they worked by making payments for it over a number of years. But each serf would not own land individually. The title to the land would be held by the mir, or village commune, to which every serf was required to belong. The communes would manage the land and collect the taxes on it.

In 1861 the serfs were freed from bondage to their masters. This meant they could no longer be bought and sold or cruelly punished by floggings. They could now leave the mir, but only with a passport. Some left to learn a trade or go into business. Those who stayed often found that the land was managed poorly by the communes; when the crop yields were low, they were unable to make their payments on the land. When food shortages resulted from the changeover, people became angry. The landowners protested that they did not get their money. The revolutionaries thought that the serfs should have been given the land outright, free of charge. The serfs felt cheated and many rioted, burned farm property, and even murdered some of the landowners.

OTHER REFORMS OF ALEXANDER

Alexander tried to improve life for other Russians. He developed railroads and introduced a banking system. He set up public courts with qualified judges and trials by juries. Some censorship was relaxed. Alexander started local government councils, elected by the people, called *Zemstvos*. Factories sprang up wherever power and resources were available. Merchants profited by their sales to the growing number of middle-class people. Russians could now become well-to-do without inheriting

The Bolshoi Theater in Moscow, where ballet is performed, was built in 1825.

money or land from their families. Education and public health were improved. More and more Russians learned how to read. Many became interested in the arts, in Paris fashions, and European ways of living.

The tsar was unable to please everyone with his reforms. He, too, was frustrated. He wanted to do his duty as ruler of a modern state, yet he felt a responsibility to keep many of the old Russian traditions, especially the power of the throne.

Many young Russians pointed out that Alexander's reforms failed to go far enough. Some revolutionary groups advocated socialism for the country. Others wanted a constitution and a republic. Some organizations tried to get the peasants to revolt.

SECRET ORGANIZATIONS

Secret terrorist organizations known as Nihilists began forming in Russia. They believed that any authoritative form of government was bad. They set out to create a new order. Their method was to throw bombs at officials and government buildings. The confusion, they thought, would cause the people to ignore the laws. Then they could take control and establish their own system. One group called the "Will of the People" tried to kill Alexander several times. Even when he left the country in 1867, a woman tried to assassinate him in Paris. Finally his luck ran out in 1881. While Alexander was riding in a carriage in St. Petersburg, a bomb was thrown in his path. The explosion killed the horses and an officer in charge of the horsemen. As Alexander got out of the carriage, another terrorist hurled a second bomb. Alexander died within an hour.

NICHOLAS II, THE LAST TSAR

Nicholas II became Russia's last tsar in 1894. He was the last of the Romanovs. Like most of the other tsars, he had an epithet—"Bloody Nicholas." His reign was marked by bloodshed from murders, riots, revolts, and wars.

RASPUTIN

Nicholas II was hardly the type of man to be a Russian emperor. He was charming but shy. He was not particularly intelligent and his greatest enjoyment came from being with his family. It was hard for Nicholas to make decisions. He was easily influenced by

Left: Tsar Nicholas II
Center: Tsarina Alexandra
Right: Rasputin

his wife, Alexandra. She, in turn, was under the spell of a strange shaggy "monk" from Siberia, named Rasputin, who was said to be a holy man able to cure people. The tsar and tsarina's little son Alexis suffered from hemophilia, a hereditary disease causing extensive bleeding from even minor injuries. Great faith was put into the healing powers of Rasputin to keep the young boy alive. Rasputin, a master of hypnotism, gained influence over Alexandra with his shrewdness, though he was usually dirty and drunk in public. Everyone hated and feared Rasputin except Alexandra, who was inspired by him, even after church leaders declared him to be a fake. He was allowed to make important decisions, even dismissing and appointing high-ranking ministers of the government.

BLOODY SUNDAY

As Rasputin's power over Nicholas and Alexandra grew, the people began to lose their respect for and confidence in the

Political convicts

imperial couple. If Nicholas realized that unrest was growing rapidly, he did little about it. When the people began to demand greater participation in making laws and sharing in the work of the government, Nicholas turned aside their requests as "senseless dreams." As autocrat of Russia, he declared, he could accept only the authority of God.

On Sunday, January 22, 1905, a priest named Father Gapon led a procession of 30,000 singing men and women to the tsar's Winter Palace. They wanted to present a petition asking for reforms, lower taxes, and better working conditions. They had hoped that Nicholas would be on hand to greet them. But he became frightened and fled the palace grounds before they arrived. The crowd carried no arms, only icons. The tsar's cossacks became alarmed at the size of the crowd and fired their guns into the mass of peaceful demonstrators. When the shooting stopped,

Crushing a demonstration on January 9, 1905

about two hundred people were killed and eight hundred wounded. Their blood poured over the square before the palace. The march was crushed on that "Bloody Sunday," but the revolutionary movement, led mainly by liberals and union workers demanding a constitution, gained sympathy and strength.

THE MARXISTS

The Marxists followed the teachings of Karl Marx, a German social and political philosopher. Their plan was to promote revolution among city workers and others of the wage-earning class of society. They were referred to as the proletariat. Marx's ideals began to appeal to many of the discontented. So did the idea of revolution. Both were to have a tremendous impact on Russia's destiny.

Above: Shooting demonstrators in Petrograd in 1917
Below: The storming of the Winter Palace

Chapter 16

RESISTERS, RIVALS, AND REVOLUTIONARIES

During the first ten years of Nicholas's reign, Russia made rapid progress in developing her industries. This was due in part to the outstanding contributions of Count Sergei Witte, a Westernized statesman who served as minister of finance. Large factories were built. Textile mills sprang up once it became profitable to use the cotton grown in the newly acquired regions of central Asia. Coal, oil, and other mineral production increased. Railroad construction continued throughout the land. In order to pay for these improvements, loans had to be obtained from abroad. Russia was especially indebted to France. Eventually repayment would have to be made.

THE RUSSO-JAPANESE WAR

With the completion of the Trans-Siberian Railroad came the advance of Russian settlers, soldiers, and commercial interests to the Far East. The wealth of China was a magnet that drew the attention of Russia to that area. China agreed to allow Russia to build a connecting railway line from the Trans-Siberian tracks to Port Arthur (Lushun) on the Yellow Sea. Japan knew Russia would now be able to use a trading port close to Korea, where Japan had hoped to make her own influence felt.

Suddenly in 1904, without declaring war, the main Japanese fleet took the Russian naval vessels stationed at Port Arthur by surprise. Many of the Russian ships in the harbor were destroyed. Japan immediately set up a blockade. The Russo-Japanese War was underway.

The European powers were unsympathetic to Russia's moves into the Far East. England even supported and cooperated with Japan. The war itself turned out to be a disaster for the Russians. Many mistakes were made. Japan won victories on land and on the sea. Russian armed forces faced the same serious problem Napoleon had faced years ago. The battlefields were much too far away from the base of supplies. It took a full fleet of Russian ships seven months to sail from the Baltic Sea, around Africa, and to the China Sea enroute to Vladivostok. Sailing through the Tsushima Strait, between southern Korea and southern Japan, the large Russian armada was attacked by the speedier and better-armed Japanese navy. In the course of a great battle, two thirds of the Russian fleet was sunk and six ships were captured. (Only four managed to escape.) Russia's hope of being master of the sea in the Far East went down with the ships.

On land the Russian and Japanese armies fought bitterly. Hundreds of thousands of men saw battle in Korea and China. The battles were long and stubborn, with very heavy casualties on both sides. By the middle of 1905, with so much unrest and antiwar feeling in Russia, and with Japan about to have a financial crisis over the cost of the war, the two countries decided to end their fighting. President Theodore Roosevelt of the United States helped bring them to the peace table. A treaty was signed at Portsmouth, New Hampshire. The end of the Russo-Japanese War halted the Russian expansion in the Far East.

WORLD WAR I

Between 1911 and 1913 a series of Balkan wars broke out. For the most part, they were confined to the region. But, on June 18, 1914, Austrian Archduke Francis Ferdinand was murdered by a Serbian man in the Bosnian town of Sarajevo. Austria at once blamed the small Slavic country of Serbia and threatened to punish her. Russia took up the cause of the little nation. Tempers flared. Threats were made by both Austria and Russia. Each displayed its military muscle while all the powers of Europe prepared for war.

Within a short time Austria declared war on Russia. The fighting quickly was joined by Germany, France, and England. Later when the United States entered, the war became worldwide.

For the Russian government, faced with fighting at home and on the field of battle, World War I was to become a disaster. The people at home were more interested in Russia's domestic problems—land ownership, industrialization, education, workers' rights, and democracy. Many showed little enthusiasm for the war effort. Russian soldiers were usually short of supplies. Perhaps one third of the huge army lacked guns and other military equipment. Nevertheless, the Russian troops fought bravely.

Though the Russian army had some success winning battles in Poland and Galicia, it was soundly beaten by the enemy in East Prussia at Tannenberg. There over 100,000 Russians were captured and tens of thousands were killed and wounded. Germany was forced to pull many of her divisions away from the western front against France in order to defeat the Russian army. Yet, during their offensives of 1915 and 1916, the Russians showed great courage against Germany's best efforts to destroy them. Still, there were many reverses and retreats. More and more Russian troops surrendered. The war dead mounted. The situation became so bad by the fall of 1915 that Tsar Nicholas, on the advice of Rasputin, took personal command of the armies in the field. Nicholas was of no help to his faltering army. His absence left to the empress and Rasputin the opportunity to run the government according to their own wishes.

DEATH OF RASPUTIN

With little going well anywhere for the Russians during World War I, hatred for Germany increased. The finger of fault was pointed at Rasputin, the German-born tsarina, and the Romanovs. The German-sounding name of St. Petersburg was changed to Petrograd. Some high nobles, thinking that Rasputin might be a secret German agent, plotted to murder him. At a palace party they placed poison in his wine, but it had little effect upon Rasputin. Then they lured him away from the reception and shot him. That, too, failed to kill him. He charged after his assassins and had to be shot again and again. Still alive after a beating, he was dumped into an icy river. Rasputin's cheating, bad influences in public affairs, and shameful private life finally came to an end on a cold December night in 1916.

With the war just about lost, with Rasputin out of the way, with large numbers of soldiers deserting, and with the Duma

RUSSIA IN 1917

— Russia's Border Today

(legislature) doing little to satisfy the needs of the people, the revolutionaries and others opposed to the government began to take matters into their own hands. The people had had their fill of wars, strikes, demonstrations, food lines, riots, and bloodshed. By 1917 they also had their fill of the autocratic Romanovs, tsars of Russia for three hundred years.

THE END OF TSARISM

When riots broke out in Petrograd during March of 1917, Nicholas II ordered troops sent there to restore order. It was too late. The soldiers refused to fire on the crowds of strikers and demonstrators. Many troop units went over to the side of the workers. The government resigned, and the Duma, supported by the army, called on the emperor to give up his power. He and his family were immediately arrested and later sent to Siberia, a fate that he had ordered for countless others. About a year later Nicholas and his family were murdered in the house in which they were being held prisoners.

Revolutionaries generally set out to bring a sudden change to the government of a country. They seek to overthrow an existing form of government, and to replace it with one having completely different ideas, purposes, methods, and ways of operating. In Russia, at this time, the revolution was to become a reality.

A government building in the Moscow Kremlin shows the European influence in architecture.

Chapter 17

RUSSIA'S CONTRIBUTION TO THE ARTS

ARCHITECTURE

The Byzantine style of architecture, with its central dome over a square space and its wall coverings of marble and mosaics, was the main type of design used in Russia from the tenth century to the beginning of the sixteenth century.

After the fall of Constantinople in 1453, Moscow began to determine Russian style. Byzantine influences gave way to the ideas of European architects, especially Italians.

Later, mostly at the start of the eighteenth century, a new era in Russian architecture began. Under the influence of Peter the Great, buildings like those found in western Europe were constructed. No longer was there a Russian national style centered in and around Moscow. Now, with St. Petersburg as the hub of the new culture, things began to change. The palaces, theaters, monuments, and government buildings frequently imitated those in Paris, Rome, Amsterdam, or Berlin.

Magnificent examples reflecting the three periods of Russian architecture—the Byzantine, the Moscow, and the St. Petersburg—remain intact throughout the country today. Some of the buildings serve as museums to exhibit and preserve Russia's proud heritage.

A few examples are the Winter Palace in St. Petersburg (now Leningrad), St. Basil's Church and the Kremlin in Moscow, and the Cathedral of St. Sophia in Kiev.

ART

Russian painting was introduced about the eleventh century. It began with painting on freshly spread wall plaster. The method was taught to the Russians by Greek artists. This kind of art, known as fresco painting, was used to decorate church walls. In time Russian artists became quite good at painting religious figures on panels, known as icons. These saintly images were usually done in blue, red, or green against a gold background, according to established patterns. The traditional style was meant to draw the viewer's mind toward sacred thoughts and eventually salvation. Some icons painted nearly seven hundred years ago are still considered masterpieces in the world of art. The most famous Russian painter of icons was Andrei Rublev. He lived from about 1370 to 1430. Many consider him to be the equal of the great masters of the early Renaissance period.

Art in Russia was set back for two centuries by the church's opposition to the painting of nonreligious subjects. By the seventeenth century the influence of Western art began to appear in Russia, and by the nineteenth century Russian artists began to paint portraits and scenes according to their own inspirations.

The great Russian painters Vereshchagin, Repin, and Vasnetsov

Left: Ilya Repin's painting of cossacks writing a letter. Right: A calendar of saints and festivals in August by an unknown Russian painter

painted historical pictures about Russia's past. Basil Vereshchagin also did many canvases showing war scenes that he observed firsthand.

Fine works by these nineteenth century masters and greatly admired works of Gay, Surikov, and others are displayed in famous galleries and museums in Moscow, Leningrad, and many other cities throughout Russia.

Russian-made art is unique in that before 1917 little sculpture of the images of man, such as figurines, or the carved or molded representations of persons, appeared as monuments or religious statues.

During the early part of the twentieth century, Russian artists excelled at producing ballet, opera, and stage scenery. They also were respected for their costumes and creative graphic arts.

Marc Chagall, Vasili Kandinsky, and other Russian artists are leaders of modern painting.

Russian composers (left to right): Tchaikovsky, Rimsky-Korsakov, and Sergei Rachmaninoff

MUSIC

Beautiful Russian music, written by outstanding composers and played by great symphony orchestras, can be heard the world over.

Before the nineteenth century Russian music received little attention. Most of it consisted of folk songs and sacred works.

In the nineteenth century a number of extremely talented composers created immortal music that will be enjoyed forever. Interest in music and music education increased. Conservatories were established in St. Petersburg, Moscow, and other cities.

Peter Tchaikovsky dominated symphonic music in the second half of the nineteenth century. Ballets for which he composed the music, such as *Swan Lake* and *The Nutcracker*, are performed by dance companies throughout the world. His "1812 Overture" celebrates the defeat of Napoleon.

Glinka, Rubinstein, Mussorgsky, Borodin, and Rimsky-Korsakov are some other prominent Russian composers.

In the twentieth century, the tradition of masterful musical composition was continued by Rachmaninoff, known for his piano compositions, Stravinsky, who wrote ballet music, and other versatile musical artists.

BALLET

Ballet is a Russian specialty that had its beginnings in dance performances given before Tsar Alexis in 1672. The first regular ballet was performed in 1735 by the dancing master of the Russian Military Academy. Later, folk dances and Russian themes became important.

In the beginning of the nineteenth century the government began to support ballet schools. Even the children of serfs were enrolled in them. Those selected were required to study ballet for at least ten years. Emphasis was placed on producing ballet stars rather than members of an ensemble.

By the late 1800s the St. Petersburg Ballet had become world famous. Thousands of young Russians made the ballet their profession. Great dancers, such as Anna Pavlova, Adolph Bolm, and Vaslav Nijinsky, helped boost Russian ballet to the foremost position in the world of dance.

LITERATURE

The greatest Russian poet of his time was Alexander Pushkin. When he was eight years old he was writing exceptional verse. His work was first published when he was fifteen. Poems and dramas like "Ode to Liberty" and *Boris Godunov* took issue with the autocratic practices of the tsars.

Michael Lermentov, another great poet produced many works

Left: Gogol   Right: Chekov and Gorky

before he was eighteen years old. Statues of Pushkin and Lermentov are appropriately placed at the entrances to many schools and libraries throughout Russia today to honor their contributions to the Golden Age of Russian Poetry.

Nikolai Gogol put excitement into his writing. He also used clever humor in some of his books and plays by poking fun at the government and some of their dishonest officials. His best novel is *Dead Souls.*

Ivan Turgenev was born rich. His family possessed five thousand serfs. His mother often had the serfs flogged or sent to Siberia when they disobeyed orders. One of Turgenev's *A Sportsman's Sketches* tells about a lonely serf forced to kill a puppy, his only friend, because its barking disturbed the landowner. Probably Turgenev is best remembered for his novel *Fathers and Sons.*

Fedor Dostoyevsky's *Crime and Punishment, The Idiot, The Possessed,* and *The Brothers Karamazov* were major contributions to Russian literature. Writing during the 1800s, Dostoyevsky mastered psychoanalysis before it was a science. He delved into the souls of his characters as no other writer had done. Dostoyevsky wrote during the period called the Golden Age of Russian Literature. Most of his books deal with poor, unhappy, or strange characters who do not fit in their society.

Vissarion Belinsky was a famous literary critic. He recognized Dostoyevsky's talent and helped make him a literary celebrity.

Count Leo Tolstoy's two great novels, *War and Peace* and *Anna Karenina*, are considered literary classics. He was the son of a Russian aristocrat. He described his early life in *Childhood, Boyhood, and Youth.* Tolstoy also wrote pamphlets and articles on social, religious, and moral themes.

During the end of the nineteenth century Anton Chekhov wrote dramas. His plays, including *The Three Sisters* and *The Cherry Orchard*, are still performed today.

Maxim Gorky, whose real name was A.M. Peshkov, wrote plays, stories, and poems. *The Lower Depths*, his most famous play, concerns derelicts in a flophouse.

RUSSIA TO 1917

It would be a mistake to judge that Russia until 1917 was simply a record of rulers and resisters, of suffering and strife, of destruction and darkness. Russia's story is much more than that. There is a brighter side. It is also a tale of development, of progress, and of glorious contributions to the arts. Brilliant Russian artists have left us with time-honored treasures of architecture, painting, music, ballet, and literature.

MINI-FACTS AT A GLANCE

GENERAL INFORMATION ON PRE-1917 RUSSIA

Official Name: The Russian Empire

Capital: St. Petersburg (renamed Petrograd in 1914)

Official Language: Russian

Other Languages: There were more than 120 separate languages and many dialects spoken in the Russian Empire, including Byelorussian, Ukrainian, Finnish, Turkic, and Yiddish.

Government: In 1916, Russia's form of government was a constitutional monarchy, which had been established after the Revolution of 1905. At the head of the government was Tsar Nicholas II, who still held most of the power of government. The Duma (legislature) and the State Council were responsible for making the laws. However, the tsar had the power of veto. In addition, the Council was more powerful than the Duma and could veto laws passed by the Duma. The Duma consisted of members elected for five years. The State Council had an equal number of elected members and members nominated by the tsar.

The Ruling Senate *(Pravitelstvuyushchiy Senat')*, established by Peter I in 1711, was the high court of justice. The Holy Synod ruled over religious affairs. All of the synod's decisions had to be approved by the tsar. The third branch of the national government was called the Council of Ministers, and included ministers of war and marine, finance, agriculture, and commerce and industry. At the provincial level were governors appointed by the tsar. Some regions were governed by governors-general, who had supreme control of all affairs, civil and military. At the village level, the village elders were more or less in charge. Constitutional monarchy in Russia had a very short and shaky existence. It provided few rights for the peasants and left the upper classes dissatisfied, also.

National Song: "God Save the Tsar" *("Bozhe tsarya khrani")* with words by V. Zhukovsky and music by A.F. Lvov.

Religion: The official religion before the October Revolution of 1917 was the Russian Orthodox faith. The Holy Synod, the ruling body of the Russian church, was established in 1721. Included in this body were the metropolitans of St. Petersburg, Moscow, and Kiev, the archbishop of Georgia (Caucasus), and several bishops. There were many other practicing churchgoers, including Roman Catholics, Lutherans, Muslims, Baptists, Buddhists, and Jews. Roman Catholics were most numerous in Poland; Lutherans lived in the Baltic area; Muslims were found in eastern and southern Russia; Jews were almost entirely settled in the towns and larger villages of western and southern provinces.

Money: The basic monetary unit in Russia was the ruble, worth 100 kopecks. There were silver and paper rubles. Gold coins known as imperials and half imperials were worth 15 and 7.5 rubles respectively. There were also paper notes worth 1, 3, 5, 10, 25, 50, 100, and 500 rubles.

Weights and Measures: Russia had her own special system of weights and measures, including the verst (3,500 feet), the sazhen (7 English feet), the arshin (28 inches), a square verst (0.439408 square miles), a dessiative (2.69972 English acres), and a pound (nine tenths of an English pound).

Calendar: The Julian Calendar, established by Julius Caesar in 46 B.C., was still in force in 1916. It is thirteen days behind the Gregorian Calendar, which the rest of Europe adopted between 1582 and 1753.

Population: 182,182,600 (1915 estimate)

Cities:

(European Russia, chiefly 1913)
Petrograd (St. Petersburg)..2,318,645
Moscow 1,817,100
Odessa 631,040
Kiev 610,190
Riga 569,100

(Poland, chiefly 1913)
Warsaw 909,491
Lodz 415,604

(Finland, chiefly 1912)
Helsingfors (Helsinki) 170,500
Åbo 54,450

(Caucasus, chiefly 1913)
Tiflis 327,800
Baku 237,000

(Siberia, chiefly 1913)
Irkutsk 129,700

(Central Asia)
Tashkent 272,300

GEOGRAPHY

Highest Point: Garmo Peak, 24,590 ft. (7,495 m), in the Russian Pamirs (now called Communism Peak)

Lowest Point: Karagiye Depression, 433 ft. (132 m) below sea level

Coastline: At no place did the Russian coastline reach the open sea. The small amount of coastline it did have was completely icebound during winter with the exception of Lapland on the north and the Black Sea on the south.

Rivers: The longest river that flows entirely within Russia is the Lena, 2,734 mi. (4,400 km) in Siberia. Other long rivers include the Amur, Ob, and Yenisey. The Volga, the longest river in Europe, is 2,194 mi. (3,531 km) long.

Lakes: The Caspian Sea, the world's largest inland body of water and a salt lake, is the largest lake. It covers 143,630 sq. mi. (372,000 km²). The largest lake entirely in Europe is Lake Ladoga, 6,835 sq. mi. (17,703 km²). The deepest lake in the world is Lake Baikal in Siberia, 5,315 ft. (1,620 m) deep.

Mountains: Russia has a number of mountain ranges, including the Carpathians, the mountains of the Caucasus and the Crimea, the Urals, the Caspians, and the Pamirs.

Climate: Because Russia is so vast, its climate varies from the Arctic in the north to subtropical zones in the south. The climate is also influenced by land features, such as the Crimean mountains that block cold air from the north. The climate of Russia is continental, which is to say summer and winter temperatures vary greatly. In Moscow, for example, the mean January temperature is 54°F. (30°C.) lower than that of July 1. The degree of continentality increases going eastward. In Yakutia, in eastern Siberia, the difference between the averages of the warmest and coldest months can be 108 to 117°F. (60 to 65°C.). The winters are very cold except in the Crimea. In western Siberia the snow stays on the ground for 140 to 260 days or more. The amount of precipitation varies from the Kara-Kum and Kyzyl-Kum deserts, where there is practically no snow cover, to West Transcaucasia, where precipitation is greater than 80 in. (203.20 cm) per year. On the mountain slopes of this region, precipitation is as high as 160 in. (406.40 cm).

Area: 8,600,000 sq. mi. (22,273,893 km^2)

NATURE:

Trees: There are many forests in the plains and the mountains of Russia, some with similar varieties of deciduous and evergreen trees. In the Russian plain: spruce, fir, Siberian spruce, oak, birch, beech, and linden. In the Caucasus: pine, spruce, fir, oak, hornbeam ash, beech, and wild fruit trees. In the subtropical zone of the Caucasus: laurel, palm, bamboo, and boxtree. In the western Siberian plain: spruce, cedar, pine, and fir. In central Siberia: Pine forests cover about 60 percent of the area. Northeastern Siberia: larch. In the Far East: stony birch, Dahurian larch, Sayan spruce, oak, hornbeam ash, Korean cedar, maple, Manchurian nut, and fir.

Fish, ocean: Siberian salmon, humpback (Pacific) salmon, herring, cod, smelt, seatrout, pike, and whitefish

Fish, inland: Carp, bream, pike, perch, and vendace

Animals and Birds: There is a great variety of animals, including the Arctic fox, sable, northern reindeer, elk, wolf, wolverine, snowy owl, lynx, hare, brown bear, wild goat, leopard, pheasant, hedgehog, white-tailed deer, squirrel, eagle, Caucasian grouse, bustard, wildcat, brindled gopher, and wild boar.

EVERYDAY LIFE:

Food: The diet of the peasant in Russia was very starchy. Pancakes called *bliny, oladii,* and *blinchiki* were very popular. Other staples of the Russian diet were cabbage dishes; soups such as borscht; grains such as cooked buckwheat, millet, and barley; dark bread; and herring. Russians, even now, prefer tea to coffee, which they drink out of glasses rather than cups. Favorite alcoholic beverages include *kvas,* a summer drink made by fermenting rye or barley, vodka, and cherry liqueur (*nalivka*). During the Russian Easter, Russians ate ham, lamb, suckling pig, multicolored eggs, *zakuski* (hors d'oeuvres), varieties of smoked and pickled fish, Easter cakes (*kulichi*), and *paskha*, a sort of pudding made of butter, cream, sugar, eggs, and cottage cheese.

Housing: In European Russia at the beginning of the twentieth century, houses in towns were often built of stone and painted white, yellow, or pink. In the suburbs, houses were of wood. In tiny villages, Russian peasants lived in one-room log cabins. A brick stove was used for heating, cooking, baking, and also as a couch and a bed. Bathing was done in a public bathhouse. On the steppes, housing was even cruder, consisting of mud or clay huts.

Holidays:

January 1	New Year's Day
January 6	Epiphany and Jordan Festival
February 2	Purification of the Virgin
March 25	Annunciation
April 23	Saint's Day of the Tsarina
May 6	Birthday of the Tsar
May 9	Festival of the Transference of the Relics of St. Nicholas the Wonder-Worker
May 14	Coronation
May 25	Birthday of the Tsarina
July 22	Saint's Day of the Dowager Empress
July 30	Birthday of the Tsarevitch Alexis Nikolayevitch
August 6	Transfiguration
August 15	Assumption
August 30	St. Alexander Nevsky
September 8	Nativity of the Virgin
September 14	Elevation of the Cross
October 1	Protection and Intercession of the Virgin
October 5	Saint's Day of the Tsarevitch
October 21	Accession of Tsar Nicholas II
October 22	Festival of the Wonder-Working Ikon of the Kazan Virgin
November 14	Birthday of the Dowager Empress
November 21	Presentation of the Virgin
December 6	Festival of St. Nicholas the Wonder-Worker and Saint's Day of the Tsar
December 25, 26, 27	Christmas

In addition to these may be mentioned the religious holidays of "Butter Week" (the week before Lent); Holy Week; Easter Sunday and Easter Week; Ascension Day; Whitsunday; and Whitmonday.

Culture: The arts flourished during the nineteenth and early twentieth centuries in almost every area—literature, drama, music, ballet, and painting. Important writers of the period included Anton Chekhov, Fedor Dostoyevsky, Alexander Pushkin, Leo Tolstoy, and Ivan Turgenev. Dostoyevsky was famous for long novels that were darkly religious and full of suffering. He dramatized the plight of the downtrodden of society. Tolstoy's themes were of family life, religion, and the changing political environment of his homeland. In music, one of the first great Russian composers of the period was Mikhail Glinka, who drew much of his material from Russian folklore. Later composers also drew on native melodies and themes. Modest P. Mussorgsky, for example, wrote the opera *Boris Godunov* in 1870 based loosely on the life of that sixteenth century tsar. Other noted Russian composers were Nicholas Rimsky-Korsakov, Peter Ilyich Tchaikovsky, Igor Stravinsky, Alexander Scriabin, and Anton Rubinstein. Dramatists popular in the later nineteenth century included Anton Chekhov and Maxim Gorky, both of whom wrote about the coarse realities of life. Several important drama groups developed in Moscow at that time. The Moscow Art Theater was the most famous. It has lasted until the present day.

Transportation: In 1917, in European Russia there were 153,782 mi. (247,486 km) of rivers, canals, and lakes. Of this, 20,670 mi. (33,265 km) were navigable for steamers, 7,482 (12,041 km) for small vessels, 88,739 (142,802 km) for rafts. In Asiatic Russia there were 86,422 mi. (139,073 km) of rivers, canals, and lakes, 21,421 (33,463 km) of which were navigable for steamers, 8,678 (13,966 km) for small sailing vessels, and 33,224 (53,469 km) for rafts. The railway system of European Russia before the revolution was nearly as large as the one in Germany. However, the proportion of railroad miles to landmass was much less in Russia. There were 35,447 mi. (57,046 km) open for traffic in January, 1912. That was one mile for every 53 sq. mi. (137 km²) of land, less than for any other European country except Norway.

Education: The Russian system of education resembled those of other European countries at the time. It began with primary school, followed by study at a middle school and then university-level training. In 1914, there were universities at Petrograd, Moscow, Kharkov, Kiev, Kazan, Odessa, Yuriev (Dorpat), Tomsk, and Saratov. The total number of students was 39,027. As of 1916, there was a women's university at Petrograd. The level of literacy in Russia was not high. In 1913, only 27 out of 100 children up to the age of nine could read.

Principal Products:
Agriculture: Wheat, rye, barley, oats, maize, corn flour, buckwheat, eggs, dairy products, sugar, fish, caviar, tobacco, horses, cattle, pigs, alcohol, gin, wines, cotton
Manufacturing: Wooden goods, metallic goods, woolens

IMPORTANT DATES

7th century B.C.—Founding of Greek colonies on the Black Sea coast; occupation of south Russian steppe by Scythians

3rd century A.D.—Goths settle on western steppes of Russia

4th century—Huns invade southern Russia

5th century—Bulgars settle middle Volga area

8th century—Khazars, a Turkish tribe, take control of the steppes, settle near the

Volga; Eastern Slavs establish themselves at Kiev in the south, Novgorod in the north, and Tmutarakan in the southeast

9th century—Cyrillic alphabet developed by Cyril and Methodius; Varangians make contact with Constantinople and keep trade route open to the south; Rurik established at Novgorod

882—Oleg founds the Russian state at Kiev

988—Conversion of Vladimir I, ruler of Kiev, to Christianity

1019-1054—First code of Russian law established during reign of Prince Yaroslav the Wise

1223—Mongols begin to conquer Rus

1240—Mongols sack Kiev; Alexander Nevsky defeats the Swedes on the Neva

1242—Alexander Nevsky defeats Teutonic knights at Lake Peipus (Lake Chudskoye)

1380—Dmitry defeats the Mongols near the river Don

1453—Constantinople captured by the Turks

1456—Moscow takes over Novgorod

1468—Ivan III marries Sophia, the only niece of the last Byzantine emperor

1558—Grigory Stroganov begins development in the east

1581—Yermak leads expedition to Siberia, defeats the Tatars

1584—Death of Ivan the Terrible; beginning of the "Time of Troubles"

1591—Dmitry, son of Ivan IV, found dead

1598—End of old dynasty; Boris Godunov becomes tsar

1601-1603—Famine

1604—False Dmitry invades Russian Ukraine

1605—Boris Godunov dies

1606—Murder of false Dmitry; Basil Shuisky becomes tsar

1608—Second false Dmitry assumes power at Moscow

1610—Poles invade Russia; Swedes take over Novgorod

1610—Second false Dmitry murdered by one of his followers

1612—Moscow and the Kremlin retaken from Poles under the leadership of Prince Pozharsky

1613—Beginning of Romanov dynasty; Mikhail Romanov becomes new tsar

1644—Poiarkov reaches the Amur River

1648—Semyon Dezhnev discovers Bering Strait

1649—*Ulozhenie* (code of laws) handed down from the tsar

1650—Yerofei Khabarov leads expedition to the Amur River

1652—Nikon, the patriarch, calls for reform of the church

1670-1671—Cossack peasant revolt led by Stepan Razin

1682—Archpriest Avvakum burned at the stake

1689—Treaty of Nerchinsk signed by China and Russia

1695—Tsar Peter I declares war on Turkey

1696—Capture of Azov

1697—Vladimir Atlasov discovers the Kamchatka peninsula that juts into the Pacific

1700—Peace with Turkey; beginning of Northern War against Sweden

1705—Beard tax

1709—Battle of Poltava

1714—Battle of Gangut, first Russian victory at sea

1710-1713—Turkish War

1721—End of Northern War

1722-23—War with Persia

1724—Vitus Bering explores Bering Strait; Catherine, Peter's wife, becomes empress

1725—Death of Peter I

1770-1774—War with Turkey

1773-1774 — Uprising led by Yemelyan Pugachov

1775 — Pugachov executed

1787 — Catherine the Great inspects Russian possessions in the Ukraine and the Crimea

1796 — Catherine dies of a stroke

1801 — Tsar Paul assassinated

1812 — Mikhail Speransky exiled; Napoleon invades Russia

1825 — Decembrist revolt crushed

1853-1856 — Crimean War

1855 — Death of Nicholas I

1861 — Alexander II frees the serfs

1864 — Russian troops wipe out rebels in Caucasus Mountains

1865-1885 — Russia establishes control over Central Asia

1867 — Russia sells Alaska to the United States

1875 — Acquisition of Sakhalin

1881 — Alexander II assassinated

1891-1905 — Trans-Siberian Railroad built

1894 — Nicholas II becomes Russia's last tsar

1904 — Japanese attack Port Arthur

1905 — "Bloody Sunday," Revolution of 1905; Treaty of Portsmouth ends war with Japan

1907 — Russia, England, and France form Triple Entente

1911-1913 — Series of Balkan wars

1914 — Outbreak of World War I

1915 — Tsar Nicholas II takes personal command of the army

1916 — Rasputin assassinated

1917 — Revolutions of March and October; Tsar Nicholas II abdicates

IMPORTANT PEOPLE

Alexander I (1777-1825), tsar

Alexander II (1818-81), tsar who freed the serfs

Alexander III (1845-94), tsar

Alexander Nevsky (c. 1220-1263), hero who defeated the Swedes and the Teutonic knights

Alexandra (1872-1918), wife of Nicholas II (executed with him)

Alexis (1690-1718), son of Peter the Great, killed by his father

Alexis (d. 1918), son of Nicholas II, executed with his family after the revolution of 1917

Vladimir Atlasov (   ), seventeenth century explorer who discovered Kamchatka

Avvakum (1621-1681), archpriest who opposed Nikon's church reforms

Basil III (1479-1533), Grand Duke of Moscow

Basil IV (Shuisky) (d. 1612), tsar during the "Time of Troubles"

Vitus Bering (1680-1741), Danish explorer who discovered the Bering Strait for Russia

Catherine I (1684?-1727), wife of Peter the Great and empress of Russia

Catherine II (1729-1796), empress of Russia, called Catherine the Great

Fedor Chaliapin (1873-1938), operatic basso

Anton Chekhov (1860-1904), dramatist and writer

St. Cyril (827-869), Apostle to the Slavs

Semyon Dezhnev (c1605-c1672), explorer of the northeastern tip of Asia

Sergei Diaghilev (1872-1929), ballet impresario

Dmitry (1582-1591), son of Ivan the Terrible

Fedor Dostoyevsky (1821-1881), novelist

Elena (   ), Ivan the Great's daughter

Elizabeth (1709-1762), empress of Russia

Fedor (1557-1598), tsar and son of Ivan the Terrible

Father Gapon (1870?-1906), led a procession during "Bloody Sunday"

Mikhail Glinka (1803-1857), composer

Boris Godunov (1551?-1605), tsar during the "Time of Troubles"

Nikolai Gogol (1809-1852), writer

Maxim Gorky (1868-1936), writer

Ivan I (d. 1340), Grand Prince of Moscow

Ivan III (1440-1505), called Ivan the Great, Grand Duke of Moscow

Ivan IV (1530-1584), called Ivan the Terrible, Grand Duke of Moscow

Vasili Kandinsky (1866-1944), painter

Yerofei Khabarov (   ), explorer of the Amur River

Mikhail Kutuzov (1745-1813), commander in chief of the Russian army against Napoleon

Marina (   ), widow of the first false Dmitry

Karl Marx (1818-1883), author, with Friedrich Engels, of *The Communist Manifesto*

St. Methodius (d. 884), Apostle to the Slavs

Modest Mussorgsky (1835-1881), composer

Nicholas I (1796-1855), tsar who crushed the Decembrists

Nicholas II (1868-1918), last tsar of Russia, executed after the 1917 revolution

Nikon (1605-1681), church reformer

Alekesi Orlov (1737-1808) and Grigori Orlov (1734-1783), coconspirators to remove Peter III from throne and replace him with his wife, Catherine

Paul (1754-1801), tsar and son of Catherine the Great

Ivan Pavlov (1849-1936), physiologist

Anna Pavlova (1885-1931), ballerina

Pavel Pestel (1795-1826), leader of the Decembrist revolt

Peter I (1672-1725), tsar, called Peter the Great, who brought Russia into the modern world

Peter III (1728-1762), tsar and husband of Catherine II

Gregory Potemkin (1739-1791), prince, one of Catherine the Great's chief advisers

Dmitry Pozharsky (1578-1642), fighter of Polish invaders during "Time of Troubles"

Yemelyan Pugachov (d. 1775), peasant rebel leader

Alexander Pushkin (1799-1837), poet

Gregory Rasputin (1872-1916), Russian monk and friend of the Empress Alexandra

Stepan Razin (d. 1671), cossack leader of peasant revolt

Ilya Repin (1844-1930), painter

Nicholas Rimsky-Korsakov (1844-1908), composer

Mikhail Romanov (1596-1645), first Romanov tsar

Anton Rubinstein (1829-1894), pianist and composer

Andrel Rublev (1370-1430), painter

Rurik (d. 879), semilegendary founder of Russia

Kondraty Ryleyev (1795-1826), poet and member of the Decembrist movement

Alexander Scriabin (1872-1915), composer

Sergius (1314?-1392?), monk and saint of the Eastern Orthodox church

Sophia (   ), wife of Ivan III

Mikhail Speransky (1772-1839), statesman who drew up a constitution and was later exiled

Igor Stravinsky (1882-1971), composer

Grigory Stroganov (   ), developer of eastern territory

Alexander Suvorov (1729-1800), general who defeated the Turks and the Poles

Peter Tchaikovsky (1840-1893), composer
Ermak Timofeyevich (Yermak) (d. 1584), conqueror in Siberia
Leo Tolstoy (1828-1910), novelist
Ivan Turgenev (1818-1883), novelist
Basil Vereshchagin (1842-1904), painter
Vladimir I (d. 1015), first Christian Grand Duke of Kiev
Vladimir II (Vladimir Monomach) (1053-1125), Grand Duke of Kiev
Sergei Witte (1849-1915), minister of finance under Nicholas II
Yaroslav (978-1054), called Yaroslav the Wise, Grand Duke of Kiev

RULERS OF RUSSIA

The First Muscovite Dynasty	Reign		
Alexander Nevsky	1252-63	Alexis	1645-76
Daniel	1276-1304	Fedor III	1676-82
Yury	1304-25	Ivan V	1682-96
Ivan I	1325-41	Peter I (the Great)	1682-1725
Simeon	1341-53	Catherine I	1725-27
Ivan II	1353-59	Peter II	1727-30
Dmitry Donskoy	1359-89	Anne	1730-40
Basil I	1389-1425	Ivan VI	1740-41
Basil II	1425-62	Elizabeth	1741-61
Ivan III (the Great)	1462-1505	Peter III	1761-62
Basil III	1505-33	Catherine II (the Great)	1762-96
Ivan IV (the Terrible)	1533-84	Paul	1796-1801
Fedor	1584-98	Alexander I	1801-25
		Nicholas I	1825-55
		Alexander II	1855-81
The Romanov Dynasty		Alexander III	1881-94
Mikhail Romanov	1613-45	Nicholas II	1894-1917

INDEX

Page numbers that appear in boldface type indicate illustrations

agriculture, 20, 21, 116
Alaska, 87, 119
Alexander I, 76, 77, 79, 81, 120
Alexander II, **90**, 91-94, 119, 120
Alexander Nevsky (Alexander of Novgorod), 35-37, **36**, 117, 121
Alexandra (wife of Nicholas II), 95, **95**, 102, 120
Alexis (son of Nicholas II), 95, 120
Alexis (son of Peter the Great), 62, 63, 120
Alexis (tsar), 50, 57, 109
alphabet, Cyrillic, **16**, 17, 117
altar Gospels, **34**
Amur River, 86, 87, 118
animals, 114
Anna Karenina, 111
Aral Sea, 87
archbishops, 29, 112
architecture, 105, 106
art, 106, 107
Arctic Ocean, 86
area, 114
Atlasov, Vladimir, 87, 118, 120
Attila, 14
Austria, 63, 67, 101
"Autocrat of All Russia," 38
Avvakum, 50, 118, 120
Azov (city), 60, 62, 118
Azov, Sea of, 26, 60
Baikal, Lake, **8**, 113
Balkans, 15, 83, 101, 119
ballet, 93, 107, 108, 109
Baltic Sea, 36, 57, 60, 62, 100
Basil III, 39, 120
Basil IV (Basil Shuisky), 45, 46, 117, 120
Batu Khan, 25
beards, 58, 118
Belinsky, Vissarion, 111
bell tower of Ivan the Terrible, **41**
Bering, Vitus, 86, 118, 120
Bering Strait, 86, 118
birch trees, **10**
birds, 114

bishops, 29, 31, 112
bishop's vestment, **31**
Black Sea, 12, 13, 32, 60, 72, 83, 113, 116
"Bloody Sunday," 95-97, 119
Bosnia, 101
Bolm, Adolph, 109
Bolshoi Theater, Moscow, **93**
Boris Godunov, 109, 116
Borodin, Alexander, 108
Borodino, Battle of, 78
boyans (minstrels), 21
boyars, 21, 22, 40, 44, 45, 58
"boyar-tsar," 46
Brothers Karamazov, The, 110
Bulgaria, derivation of word, 15
Bulgars, 15, 116
Byelorussians (White Russians), 23
Byzantine Empire, 17, 18, 22
Byzantine style of architecture, 105, 106
caftans, 58
calendar, 113
calendar of saints and festivals, **107**
capital, 112
"Cap of Monomach," **56**
Carpathian, Mountains, 15
Caspian Sea, 53, 62, 113
Cathedral of St. Sophia, Kiev, 20, 106
Cathedral of the Annunciation, 34
Cathedral of the Archangel Michael, 48
Catherine I, 65, 118, 120
Catherine II (Catherine the Great), 54, 55, 65, **66**, 67-73, 75, 119, 120
Catholicism, 18, 19, 36, 38, 45, 112
Caucasus Mountains, **13**, 87, 119
ceiling, Hermitage Museum, **69**
Chagall, Marc, 107
chalice, gold, **48**
chalice, silver, **33**
Charles XII (king of Sweden), 60

Chekov, Anton, **110**, 111, 115, 116, 120
Cherry Orchard, The, 111
Childhood, Boyhood, and Youth, 111
China, 7, 28, 87, 99, 100, 118
China Sea, 100
Christianity, 14, 17, 18-20, 27, 28, 83, 117
chronology, 116-119
Chudskoye, Lake, 36, 117
churches, **5**, 20, 22, **28**, 30, **30**, 31, **33**, 106
climate, 114
clothing, 21, 22, **54**, 58
coastline, 113
coat of chain mail, **42**
commune (mir), 92
composers, 108, 116
Constantine (brother of Tsar Alexander I), 81
Constantine (Byzantine emperor), 22
Constantinople, 17, 18, 19, 23, 27, 29, 60, 72, 105, 117
constitution, 76, 93, 97
convicts, 88, 89, **96**
cossacks, 43, 45, 46, 52-55, **53**, 85, 86, 87, 88, 96, **107**, 118
Crimea, 60, 71, 72, 83, 84, 119
Crime and Punishment, 110
Crimean Peninsula, 83
Crimean Tatars, 39
Crimean War, 83, 85, 91, 119
cross, gold, **64**
Crusaders, 23
culture, 115, 116
Cyril, 17, 117, 120
Cyrillic alphabet, **16**, 17, 117
dance, 93, 107, 108, 109,
dates, important, 116-119
Dead Souls, 110
Decembrist rebels, 82, 119
demonstrators, revolutionary, **97**, **98**
Denmark, 39, 68
Dezhnev, Semyon, 86, 118, 120
Diderot, 69

Dmitry (prince of Moscow), 27, 117
Dmitry (son of Ivan the Terrible), 44, **52**, 117, 120
Dmitry, false, 44, 45, 117
Dmitry, new, 45, 46, 117
Dnieper River, 20, 72
domes, church, onion-shaped, 30, **30**
Don cossacks (*see also* cossacks), 53-55, **53**
Don River, 27, 60, 117
Dostoyevsky, Fedor, 83, 110, 111, 115, 120
Duma, 102, 103, 112
eagle, double-headed, **90**
Eastern church, 17, 29
education, 116
"1812 Overture," 108
Elizabeth (empress), 68, 120
England, 40, 49, 73, 76, 77, 100, 101, 119
false Dmitry, 44, 45, 117
farming, 20, 21, 116
Fathers and Sons, 110
Fedor, 43, 44, 120
fiefs, 51
Finland, Gulf of, 65
Finns, 15
fish, 114
food, 114
forestlands, 12, 52
France, 22, 73, 76-79, 81, 83, 99, 101, 102, 119
Francis Ferdinand (Austrian Archduke), 101
Frederick the Great, 67
frescoes, **20**, 106
Galicia, 101
Gangut, Battle of, 61, 118
Gapon, Father, 96, 120
Gay (artist), 107
Genghis Khan, 26
geography, 113
Germans, 15, 36, 37, 38
Germany, 49, 67, 68, 77, 81, 101, 102
Glinka, Mikhail, 108, 116, 120
Godunov, Boris, 42-45, 117, 120
Gogol, Nikolai, 110, **110**, 120
Golden Gate of Kiev, **19**

Golden Horde, 25, 26, 28
Gorky, Maxim (A.M. Peshkov), **110**, 111, 116, 120
Goths, 14, 116
government, 112
Grand Army of Napoleon, 78, 79, **79**
grand princes of Moscow (Moscovy), 27, 28, 37, 39
Grand Principality (Kiev), 23
Great Britain, 58, 83
Great Russians, 23
Greece, 22
Greek Orthodoxy, 19
Greeks, 11, 12, 116
helmet, Russian, **26**
helmet, steel, **42**
Hermitage Museum (Winter Palace), 63, **66, 69,** 70, 82, 96, **98**, 106
highest point, 113
holidays, 115
Holland, 49, 58
Holy Roman Empire, 39
housing, 21, **47, 88,** 115
Hungary, 22, 39
Huns, 14, 116
Ice, Battle on the, 36, **36**, 37
icons, **30**, 31, **70**, 106
Idiot, The, 110
Imperial Guards, 68, 71, 76
India, 78
Indo-European people, 12
Iran, 12
Istanbul (Constantinople), 17
Italy, 76, 77
Ivan I (Ivan the Moneybag), 27, 120
Ivan III, 37-39, **41**, 117, 120
Ivan IV (Ivan the Terrible), 34, 39-43, **40, 41,** 73, 86, 117, 120
Ivan V, 59
Ivan the Terrible and His Son (painting), **40**
Japan, 100, 101, 119
Jewish religion, 14, 19, 112
Kamchatka peninsula, 87, 118
Kandinsky, Vasili, 107, 120
Khabarov, Yerofei, 86, 118, 120
Khazars, 14, 116
Khivans, 87

Kiev, 15, 18, 19, 20, 22, 23, 26, 72, 106, 113, 117
Kiev, Golden Gate of, **19**
Kievan Rus, 20, 22, 23
Kirghiz, 14
Korea, 100
Kremlin, Moscow, 27, **28**, 34, **41**, 46, **52**, 54, **104**, 106, 118
Kutuzov, Mikhail, 78, 79, 120
Ladoga, Lake, 113
lakes, **8**, 113
languages, 12, **16**, 17, 112
laws, first code, 22, 117
laws, new code, (1649), 50, 118
Leningrad, 59, 63, 65, 106, 107
Lermentov, Michael, 109, 110
Listvyanka, **8**
literature, 109-111, 115
Lithuania, 38, 41
Little Russians (Ukrainians), 23
log cabin, Siberia, **88**
Lower Depths, The, 111
lowest point, 113
"Mad Tsar," 73
maps of Russia:
  expansion in Asia, **84**
  expansion in Europe, **74**
  Russian Empire, 1900, **1**
  topography, **2**
Maria Feodorovna (wife of Tsar Paul), **75**
Mariinsk, Siberia, **89**
Marina (widow of false Dmitry), 46, 121
Marx, Karl, 97, 121
Marxists, 97
mercenaries, 18
Methodius, 17, 117, 121
metropolitans, 29, 112
Middle Ages, 29, 51
mir (village commune), 92
moats, town, 20
Mohammedans, 19
Moldavia, 39
Monastery of the Trinity, 32
money, 112
Mongolia, 87
Mongols, 14, 25-29, 35, 117
monks, 32, 88
Moscow, 10, 23, 26, 27, 28, 32, 34, 37, 38, 39, 40, **41**, 45, 46,

47, **52**, 54, 55, 58, 78, 79, 84, 86, 88, 89, **93, 104**, 105, 106, 107, 108, 113, 114, 117, 118
Moscow style of architecture, 105, 106
Moskva River, **52**
"Mother Russia," 7-9, 46
mountains, **13**, 114
Muscovy, 37, 51
music, 108, 116
Mussorgsky, Modest, 108, 116, 121
Napoleon Bonaparte, 73, 76-79, 100, 108, 119
Near East, 83
Nerchinsk, 87, 118
Neva River, 35, 117
new Dmitry, 45, 46, 117
Nicholas I, 81-84, 119, 121
Nicholas II, 94, 95, **95**, 96, 99, 102, 103, 112, 119, 121
Nihilists, 94
Nijinsky, Vaslav, 109
Nikon, 50, 118, 121
nomadic tribes, 11, 12, 14, 29
North America, 86, 87
Northern War, 60, 118
Norway, 22
Novgorod, 15, 18, 23, 24, 28, 35, 37, 38, 46, 85, 117
Nutcracker, The (ballet), 108
Odessa, 113
"Ode to Liberty," 109
"Old Believers," 50
Oleg, 18, 117
oprichniks, 40
Orlov, Alekesi, 68, 75, 121
Orlov, Grigori, 68, 121
Orthodox church (*see* Russian Orthodox church)
ostrogs (fortresses), 86
Our Lady of Tenderness (painting), **24**
Pacific Ocean, 8, 86, 87, 89
painting, 106, 107
Palestine, 83
parade carriage, Peter the Great's, **63**
Paris, France, 94
patriarchs, 29, 31, 47, 50
Paul (tsar), 73, 75, **75**, 76, 119,

121
Pavlova, Anna, 109, 121
peasant house, **47**
peasants, 21, 22, 32, 36, 37, 41, 43, 45, 46, 50, 51-55, 58, 75, 76, 93
people, during reign of Nicholas I, **80**
people, important, list of, 120-122
Persia, 7, 53, 62, 118
Pestel, Pavel, 82, 121
Peter I (Peter the Great), 57-65, **59, 61**, 67, 73, 105, 112, 118, 121
Peter III, 65, 67, 68, 75, 121
Peter III (pretender), 55
Peter and Paul Cathedral, **65**
Petrograd (St. Petersburg), 57, 62, 65, 68, 70, 79, 82, 94, **98**, 102, 103, 105, 106, 108, 112, 113
poetry, 109-111
Poiarkov, 86, 118
Poland, 22, 38, 39, 41, 43, 44, 45, 46, 47, 49, 62, 71, 72, 79, 101, 112, 118
Poltava, Battle of, 61, **61**, 118
population figures, 113
Port Arthur (Lushun), 100, 119
Portsmouth, New Hampshire, 101, 119
Possessed, The, 110
Potemkin, Gregory, 71, **71**, 72, 75, 121
Pozharsky, Dmitry, 46, 47, 118, 121
prehistory, 11
priests, 31, 32, 83, 96
primogeniture, 75
princes, 21, 23, 25, 27, 28, 32
products, principal, 116
proletariat, 97
Prussia, 67, 75, 101
Prut River, 62
Pugachov, Yemelyan, **54**, 55, 119, 121
Pushkin, Alexander, 109, 110, 115, 121
Rachmaninoff, Sergei, 108
railroads, 89, **89**, 99, 100, 116,

119
Rasputin, 95, **95**, 102, 119, 121
Razin, Stepan, 53, 54, **54**, 118, 121
religion, 14, 15, 17, 18-20, 27, 28, 29-32, 50, 106, 112
Religious Procession to Kursk Guverniya (painting), **9**
Renaissance, 35
Repin, Ilya, 9, 40, 106, 107, 121
Riga, 113
Rimsky-Korsakov, Nicholas, 108, **108**, 116, 121
River Kalka, Battle of the, 26
rivers, **6**, 7, 8, 113, 116
Roman Catholicism, 18, 19, 36, 38, 45, 112
Romanov, Mikhail, 47, 118, 121
Romanov dynasty, 47, 94, 103, 118
Romans, 12, 14
Roosevelt, Theodore, 101
Rubinstein, Anton, 108, **108**, 116, 121
Rublev, Andrei, 106, 121
rulers of Russia, list of, 122
Rurik, 18, 44, 117, 121
Rus (Russia), 18, 117
Russia, origin of word, 11
Russian Military Academy, 109
Russian Orthodox church, 28, 29-32, 36, 38, 46, 50, 83, 105, 112
Russo-Japanese War, 99-101
Ryleyev, Kondraty, 82, 121
St. Basil's Church, Moscow, 106
St. John the Evangelist, **33**
St. Peter and Paul Fortress, 82
St. Petersburg (Petrograd), 57, 62, 65, 68, 70, 79, 82, 94, **98**, 102, 103, 105, 106, 108, 112, 113
St. Petersburg Ballet, 109
St. Petersburg style of architecture, 105, 106
Sarajevo, Bosnia, 101
Sardinia, 83
Scandinavia, 18
Scythians, 12, 116
Sea of Azov, 26, 60
seasons, **6**

Serbia, 101
serfs, 8, 9, 19, 41, 43, 45, 51-55, 75, 77, 91, 92, 109, 110, 119
Sergius, 32, 121
Sevastopol, 83
Shamanism, 15
Shuisky, Basil (Basil IV), 45, 46, 117, 120
Siberia, 8, 15, 25, 41, 44, 52, 82, 83, 85-89, **89**, 95, 103, 110, 113, 114, 117
Sibir (city), 86
Slavs, 9, 15, 17, 18, 20, 117
sleigh, **6**
Smolensk, 46
socialism, 93
song, national, 112
Sophia (regent), 59
Spain, 77
Speransky, Mikhail, 76, 77, 119, 121
Sportsman's Sketches, A, 110
steppe lands, 8, 11, 12, 85, 116
Stone Age, 8
Stravinsky, Igor, 109, 116, 121
streltsy, 59, **59**
Stroganov, Grigory, 85, 117, 121
Surikov, V., 59, 107
Suvorov, Alexander, 71, 76, 121
Suzdal, 23
Swan Lake (ballet), 108
Sweden, 35, 43, 45, 46, 49, 60-62, 117, 118
taiga, 85
Tannenberg, East Prussia, 101
Tatars, 39, 86, 117
taxes, 12, 25, 27, 28, 29, 49, 51, 52, 58, 92
Tchaikovsky, Peter, 108, **108**, 116, 121

temperatures, 114
Teutonic knights, 35-37, 117
Third Department (secret police), 83
Three Sisters, The, 111
throne room, Peter the Great's, **63**
"Time of Troubles," 43, 49, 117
Timofeyevich, Ermak (Yermak), 86, **88**, 117, 122
Tmutarakan, 15, 117
Tolstoy, Leo, 111, 115, 122
tomb, Peter the Great, **65**
tomb, Prince Yaroslav the Wise, **20**
Transbaikalia Railroad, **89**
transportation, 116
Trans-Siberian Railroad, 89, 99, 100, 119
trees, **10**, 11, 114
Triple Entente, 119
tsar, divinity of, 50
tsar, first, 40
tsar, last, 94
tsar, symbol of, **90**
tsars, list of, 122
Tsushima Strait, 100
Turgenev, Ivan, 110, 115, 122
Turkey, 39, 41, 60, 61, 62, 71, 72, 83, 101, 118
Turkish War, 61, 118
Turko Mongols, 14
Turks, 14, 15, 27, 116, 117
Ukraine, 38, 72, 82, 117, 119
Ukrainian national costume, **4**
Ukrainians (Little Russians), 23
United States of America, 87, 101, 119
Ural Mountains, 32, 86
Ussuri River, 87

Varangians (Vikings), 18, 117
Vasnetsov, V., 41, 106
veil, showing St. John the Evangelist, **33**
Vereshchagin, Basil, 106, 107, 122
Vikings (Varangians), 18, 117
Vladimir I, 19, **19**, 117, 122
Vladimir II (Vladimir Monomach), 22, 23, 122
Vladimir (town), 23
Vladivostok, 89, 100
Volga cossacks, 85
Volga River, 14, 53, 55, 113
Voltaire, 69
War and Peace, 111
weather, 114
weights and measures, 113
White Russians (Byelorussians), 23
White Sea, 32
"Will of the People," 94
winter, 78, 79, 114
Winter Palace (Hermitage Museum), 63, **66, 69**, 70, 82, 96, **98**, 106
Witte, Sergei, 99, 122
World War I, 101, 102, 119
writers, 109-111, 115
Yaroslav the Wise, Prince, 20, 22, 117, 122
Yellow Sea, 100
Yermak (Ermak Timofeyevich), 86, **88**, 117, 122
Zakharina, Anastasia, 40
Zemstvos (government councils), 92

About the Author

Abraham Resnick, a native New Jerseyan, is a noted author and educator specializing in elementary and secondary social studies education. As a teacher of teachers Dr. Resnick has had an outstanding career as a professor, writer, supervisor, consultant, and professional leader in the social sciences. His writings include text and trade books for children, teachers' editions of school materials, published resource units, map transparencies, and professional books and articles.

The author enlisted in the armed forces during World War II, serving as a weatherman in the United States Army Air Corps.

Dr. Resnick's graduate work was completed at Teachers College, Columbia University in New York and Rutgers—The State University of New Jersey. He has received two writing awards from the National Council for Geographic Education as well as numerous other honors. He is presently serving as Professor of Education at Jersey City State College (New Jersey) and for many years was the Director of the Instructional Materials Center, Rutgers Graduate School of Education. In 1975 he was the recipient of that school's Alumni Award for Distinguished Service to Education.

When he isn't writing or teaching Abe Resnick enjoys watching professional sporting events, playing tennis, long distance walking, bike riding, and travel to remote regions of the world.